Styling Success : How to Build a Wardrobe That Reflects Your Ambitions

Gordon Mills

Published by Shirley Love, 2024.

While every precaution has been taken in the preparation of this book, the publisher assumes no responsibility for errors or omissions, or for damages resulting from the use of the information contained herein.

STYLING SUCCESS : HOW TO BUILD A WARDROBE THAT REFLECTS YOUR AMBITIONS

First edition. September 1, 2024.

Copyright © 2024 Gordon Mills.

ISBN: 979-8227771537

Written by Gordon Mills.

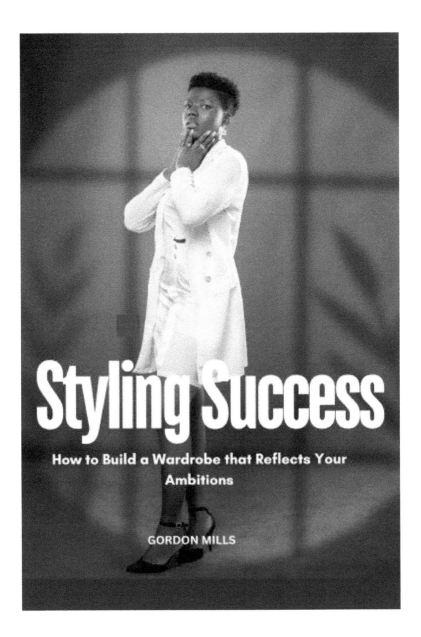

GORDON MILLS

STYLING SUCCESS

How to Build a Wardrobe that Reflects Your Ambitions

STYLING SUCCESS : HOW TO BUILD A WARDROBE THAT REFLECTS YOUR AMBITIONS

GORDON MILLS

Dedication

To Princella,
    Your style isn't just something you wear—it's a reflection of who you are, and that's what I admire most about you. Watching you express yourself through fashion, I've come to realize that clothes can be more than just fabric; they can be a powerful statement of confidence, ambition, and individuality. This book is a journey into understanding that very idea—a journey you've inspired.

Your elegance, your ability to make any outfit your own, and the way you carry yourself with such poise have all been a constant source of inspiration for me. It's not just about how you look; it's about how you make others feel with your presence, your warmth, and your undeniable sense of self.

In writing this book, I wanted to capture that essence—the idea that style is deeply personal, yet universally impactful. I've poured into these pages everything I've learned from observing your grace and how it connects with the way you move through the world. It's more than a guide; it's a tribute to the way you've shown me that fashion isn't just about appearances—it's about embracing who you are and letting the world see it too.

This book is born from the admiration I have for you—your grace, your elegance, and the effortless way you make style your own. Your presence is a reminder that fashion isn't just about clothes, but about the confidence and beauty you bring to the world. You've inspired every page of this journey, and I'm forever grateful for the way you've shown the true art of expressing oneself through appearance. This is for you, with deep admiration and respect.

This book is as much yours as it is mine. Thank you for being the inspiration behind it and for showing me the true art of dressing with purpose and pride.

Introduction

You have to admit, girl, that your attire is your first line of protection. It resembles your shield, your seal of approval, and announcing to the world, "This is me, and I'm here to slay." Now, I'm not suggesting that you just wear whatever is fashionable or clean. No, it goes beyond that. Your clothes are your visual CV. Your clothing tell a story about you before you even speak a word when you enter into a room. You want them to say all the right things, I promise.

When I think about style, the first person who comes to mind is Princella. She's someone who embodies everything this book is about—effortless elegance, unshakable confidence, and a sense of self that radiates through every outfit she wears. Watching her express herself through fashion, I've come to understand that clothes are more than just fabric; they're a powerful extension of who we are, a reflection of our ambitions, our dreams, and our identity.

This book was born out of my admiration for her. It's not just about the clothes we choose to wear, but about how those choices shape the way we present ourselves to the world. Princella has taught me that true style goes beyond trends; it's about knowing who you are and letting that guide your wardrobe. It's about making decisions that align with your goals and aspirations, and that's the journey I want to take you on with this book.

In the pages that follow, we'll explore how to build a wardrobe that isn't just stylish, but meaningful—one that reflects your ambitions and helps you step into every room with confidence. Whether you're

STYLING SUCCESS : HOW TO BUILD A WARDROBE THAT REFLECTS YOUR AMBITIONS

dressing for success in the workplace, curating a collection of timeless pieces, or learning the art of accessorizing, this book will guide you in making choices that align with your personal style and career goals.

Princella's influence runs through every chapter of this book. Her ability to make any outfit her own, to carry herself with grace and poise, has shown me that fashion isn't just about looking good—it's about feeling good, too. It's about the quiet power that comes from knowing you're presenting your best self to the world, every single day.

This book is a tribute to that philosophy. It's for anyone who wants to understand the deeper connection between style and self-expression, who wants to build a wardrobe that speaks to who they are and where they're going. Whether you're just starting to find your style or you're looking to refine it, I hope this book will inspire you to embrace the power of fashion as a tool for achieving your ambitions.

So, as you read through these pages, remember that style is personal, it's powerful, and it's yours to define. Let this book be your guide, and let Princella's elegance and confidence inspire you as much as they've inspired me.

SO LET'S GET REAL: style is subjective. It's okay if what suits me doesn't suit you; after all, style isn't universal. Finding what helps you feel better about yourself is the key. Ever notice how a well-chosen ensemble can instantly lift your spirits? Like, all of a sudden, you're untouchable the moment you put on those shoes and zip up that dress. That is style's power. It's more than just appearances—it's about feeling invincible. It's about knowing that you look as tough as you feel and stepping into any scenario with your head held high.

LET'S BE HONEST. FASHION isn't just for movie stars or runway models. It's for the average woman who wants to express herself and take control of her workspace—be it an office, a classroom, or any other place. To appear wealthy, you don't need to have a million dollars. It all comes down to learning how to accessorize, mix and match, and—above all—wear your confidence like the greatest accessory you can wear.

"But I'm not a fashion expert; I have no idea where to start when it comes to building a wardrobe," you may be thinking. You don't have to be, girl. All you really need is self-awareness, an understanding of your personal fulfillment, and a willingness to take some risks. That's where I enter the picture. I'll grab your hand and we'll work together to construct that wardrobe. We'll determine what suits you, what gives you a sense of strength, and what purchases you should make to ensure that you always look your best.

Let's now discuss the relevance of this. For it's not just about looking adorable here. This is about living your life with intention. It's important to dress for the life you desire rather than the one you now lead. Do you want to be in charge? Put on attire appropriate for it. Do you want respect and credibility? Put on attire appropriate for it. Do you want to be the most confident woman in the room? Put on attire appropriate for it. Clothing has the power to alter how you view yourself and, more significantly, how other people see you.

SURE, WE'VE ALL EXPERIENCED those days. After getting out of bed, put on clean clothes and hope no one sees that you're still half asleep. On the other hand, there are days when you take your time, choose your attire, and feel ready to take on the world as soon as you leave the house. Here, that's the emotion we're pursuing. I want you to experience more of those days and those "Damn, I got this" moments when you look in the mirror.

STYLING SUCCESS : HOW TO BUILD A WARDROBE THAT REFLECTS YOUR AMBITIONS

YOUR CLOSET SERVES as both a creative canvas and a playground, allowing you to express yourself to the fullest. You don't have to try to fit in with other people's ideas of what's fashionable or chase after every trend. This is about you and the kind of person you wish to be in the world. And believe me when I say that nothing is more powerful than a woman who owns and understands her sense of style.

HOWEVER, BEFORE WE get started creating that dream wardrobe, we must discuss mindset. Because, honey, it won't matter if you have the most amazing clothes in the world if your mental health isn't in good shape. Self-perception is the foundation of confidence. It won't matter what you're wearing if you don't feel good about yourself. Thus, we will also work on that. After we clear your mental clutter, you'll be able to wear your power, confidence, and ambition when you step out in that outfit.

NOW, I'M NOT SAYING that clothes are everything. Of course, you need to have the talents, the brains, and the hustle to back it all up. But when you look nice, you feel good, and when you feel good, you do good. It's all connected. Your style is just one piece of the puzzle, but it's a crucial one. It's the element that links everything else together and makes you feel like the boss you are.

So let's talk about the essentials. We're gonna start with the foundation of your wardrobe, those crucial pieces that you can build on, mix and match, and wear in a million different ways. We're talking about that perfect pair of pants, that little black dress, that blazer that fits just exactly. These are the pieces that every woman needs, no matter her style. And don't worry, I'm not going leave you hanging. I'm gonna break it all down for you, step by step, so you know exactly what to look for and how to make it work for you.

But we're not stopping there. We're gonna get into the fun stuff too—accessories, shoes, luggage, the works. Because girl, the perfect accessories can elevate your outfit from "meh" to "wow" in seconds. And I'm gonna show you how to accomplish it without breaking the bank. It's all about being wise with your money, understanding when to splurge and when to save, and making sure that every piece you buy adds value to your wardrobe.

NOT TO BE OVERLOOKED are the last details. Since style is more than simply what you wear, it also involves how you wear it. It all comes down to attitude, confidence, and the realization that you look amazing. We will discuss how to wear red lipstick without feeling like it is too much, how to walk like you were born in heels, and how to make sure that every time you step out, you do it in style.

ARE YOU PREPARED NOW? Are you prepared to elevate your fashion game and create a wardrobe that embodies both your desired identity and identity now? Because, believe me when I say this, everything else just falls into place once you start dressing with intention and putting together looks that make you feel like the best version of yourself. Everyone begins to perceive you and yourself in a different light.

STYLING SUCCESS : HOW TO BUILD A WARDROBE THAT REFLECTS YOUR AMBITIONS

This book isn't about attempting to fit in with someone else's definition of style or the newest trends. The key is to discover your unique voice and style and use them to convey who you are to the outside world. It's about knowing that you're prepared for whatever the day has in store for you as you walk out the door, feeling good about yourself, and your attire.

LET'S GET STARTED. Together, we can create the ideal wardrobe, discover your personal style, and ensure that you draw attention whenever you enter a space. It's time to stop hiding behind garments that don't make you feel fantastic and to quit acting small. It's time to start dressed like the confident, assertive woman you are—a woman who knows what she wants and doesn't back down from a challenge.

Recall that fashion is a journey rather than a destination. Thus, go slowly, enjoy yourself, and don't be scared to take some chances. Because wearing what makes you feel good is the only guideline that matters when it comes to fashion. All other things are merely sounds.

Chapter 1

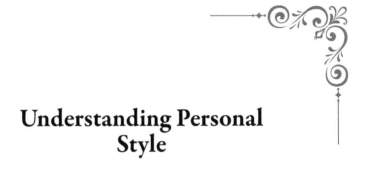

Understanding Personal Style

Now, let's discuss the most crucial aspect of this entire style journey: **YOU**. Yes, I'm referring to the genuine you—the individual with a distinct personality, style, and manner of presenting herself to the world. Disregard what your closest buddy is wearing, what the mags say, and what's popular on Instagram. This is about discovering your personal style and how to express it via your wardrobe. Because, believe me, everything else just falls into place once you connect with your own style.

Identifying Your Style Personality

Discovering what your current wardrobe says about you.

First things first, girl—we need to closely examine the materials you are currently using. I want you to truly open that closet. Step back and observe what transpires inside. How does it feel? Is everything neutral here? Are there sporadic bursts of color? More stilettos or sneakers, in your opinion? Is everything in disarray or is everything well-organized? Your current outfit speaks volumes about who you are, or at least who you believe yourself to be, sis.

You see, the things you are wearing now have a narrative. Perhaps it's a tale you were telling without even realizing it. Perhaps you're not very excited about the story. The problem is that your wardrobe acts as a mirror, reflecting back your habits, personality, and emotional state. You may be the adventurous kind that loves to try new things and wears everything that catches your eye. Perhaps you're the kind who stays true to what's basic, keeping things elegant and straightforward. In any case, those outfits capture who you are right now. Even though it's not a complete picture, they are presenting the world with your self-image.

NOW PAUSE TO CONSIDER what your clothing is trying to tell you. Do you feel at ease with it? Does it represent who you wish to be? Is it more of a case of "I wear this because it's what I've always worn" mentality? It's time for you to be honest with yourself, girl. Here, facts

STYLING SUCCESS : HOW TO BUILD A WARDROBE THAT REFLECTS YOUR AMBITIONS

are presented without bias. It's okay if you have a lot of vintage t-shirts and cozy sweatshirts in your closet, but is it really who you are? Is that the kind of person you want to be every day? It might be or it might not be. In any case, let's begin here. We will decipher the meaning sent by your clothing and, if necessary, alter the narrative.

Finding inspiration from style icons and fashion trends

Now that we know what your wardrobe has been trying to tell you, let's get some ideas. And believe me when I say that there is an abundance of stuff available. A full world of fashion is at your fingertips with style symbols, trends, and Instagram feeds. However, keep in mind that just because something looks beautiful on Beyoncé or Rihanna, it doesn't always imply it will work on you. That's alright, too! Instead than trying to emulate someone else's style, the idea is to pick elements that speak to you and transform them into something uniquely your own.

Consider who motivates you to begin. It might be a famous person, a friend, or that girl you see every morning at the coffee shop who always seems put together. What draws your attention to their style? Is it how they blend patterns together? the effortless elegance with which they usually manage to dress? How do they take chances with their attire? Observe it, whatever it may be. It's providing you with hints about what you could want to use in your own style.

AND NOW, LET'S HAVE a little discussion on fashion trends. Trends are definitely entertaining. They offer an opportunity to venture beyond your comfort zone and attempt something new. But avoid becoming overly engrossed in them. Something doesn't necessarily have to be in your closet just because it's "in." While trends change over time, your own style never goes out. Thus, follow a trend if it appeals to you. If it doesn't, move on to something else. It's okay to cling to what makes sense for you.

Here's the catch, though: you have to personalize it. Take those trends and that inspiration, and make them uniquely your own. Perhaps you think high-waisted jeans are so cute, but you're not sure how they look on you. That's awesome! Experiment with different colors, fabrics, and cuts. It's important to wear something that makes you feel good about yourself. It isn't correct if it seems forced. If you think you're exerting too much effort, take a step back and evaluate. Rather than seeming like you're dressing up, your style should feel like a natural extension of who you are.

Aligning your style with your lifestyle and career goals

Let's now discuss the pragmatic aspects of the situation. Because, really, lady, what good is it to have the coolest wardrobe in the world if it doesn't fit your lifestyle? Your style ought to complement you rather than contradict you. Now, let's talk honestly about your daily activities. Do you work nine to five in an office? Do you spend your entire day chasing after children? Are you working incredibly hard to land freelance jobs? Your clothing should be able to fit into whatever shape your life takes on.

Imagine a normal day in your life. How are you spending your time? With whom are you seeing? To what destination are you heading? That should be reflected in the clothes you wear. If you work for a corporation, you could require more polished, formal writing. However, it doesn't mean you have to lead a dull life. Your professional attire nevertheless allows you to express your individuality. Perhaps it's a striking necklace, a coat, or a pair of amazing heels. The secret is striking a balance between remaining authentic and projecting a professional image.

It's also okay if you lead a more laid-back lifestyle. However, carefree need not equate to careless. You may be at ease and still look put together. Finding the things that not only fit into your daily routine but also uplift your mood is the key. Perhaps it's a stylish sneaker,

STYLING SUCCESS : HOW TO BUILD A WARDROBE THAT REFLECTS YOUR AMBITIONS

a warm jacket, or a fantastic pair of trousers. Make sure you feel comfortable doing whatever it is.

However, we're not merely discussing the present. We're also discussing your future plans. What objectives do you have? In five years, where do you see yourself? Your clothes can guide you in that direction. Don't dress for the job you have; dress for the one you want. Start dressed like you already have a promotion if you're aiming for one. When starting your own firm, present yourself as the boss that you are. Not only can your wardrobe influence how people perceive you, but it may also influence how you view yourself. You begin to attract the life you want when you begin to dress for it.

HERE'S THE THING: HAVING a stylish appearance isn't the only aspect of personal style. It's about dressing to fit your life and your objectives, feeling good about yourself, and being authentic. It's about feeling like the best version of yourself every day when you leave your house. It's about knowing that you're presenting the true you—the self-assured, competent, and world-ready version of yourself—when you enter that meeting, that date, or that celebration.

YOUR STRENGTH IS YOUR style, girl. It's how you express who you are to the world without ever speaking. Own it, then. Accept it. Most importantly, enjoy yourself while doing it. Because you exude confidence in everything you do when you feel good about what you're wearing. And therein lies the true key to successful styling, my friend.

That's the real deal when it comes to knowing your own style. It all comes down to you, your style, and your objectives; make sure your clothing reflects all of that. We have a lot more to discover, so for now, just take a moment to gather your thoughts, let everything sink in, and get ready to start creating a wardrobe that is uniquely you. We're only getting started. Because you ought to present yourself every day in your finest, most fashionable form. And believe me, people are eager to see what you have to give.

The Psychology of Fashion

Clothes are made of more than just fabric, as we are all aware. They serve as more than just a means of warmth and concealment. Clothing has power, ladies. They have the power to influence our thoughts, feelings, and even behaviors. It's genuine and profound. Now that you know that what you wear can alter your entire mood, let's explore the psychology of fashion. It's time to start taking advantage of this.

How clothing influences your confidence and mood?

Let's start by talking about confidence. Have you ever noticed your emotional state when wearing something you adore? I mean, the look that gives you a little more confidence, makes you walk with a little more swagger, and makes you smile like you're crushing it. Girl, that's not just in your brain. The relationship between clothing and confidence is a complex psychological phenomenon.

Wearing something that makes you feel wonderful is like turning on an internal switch. All of a sudden, you're the greatest version of yourself—not just you. You're prepared to take on the world and enter any space as though it were your own. It seems as though what you're wearing gives you the go-ahead to be brave, noticeable, and authentically you. And that, darling, is the power of style. It functions as a kind of personal armor that lets you declare, "I'm here and I'm ready for whatever comes my way."

However, it goes beyond that. Your mood might also be affected by your wardrobe. Have you ever worn something that seems strange? For example, does it feel unnaturally tight, is the color off, or is it just too tight? It's similar to having a cloud over your head all day. You seem unable to be who you truly are, and you're squirming and uncomfortable. This is so because your clothing choices directly reflect your feelings. It's obvious when you're not feeling what you're wearing. It has an impact on your gait, speech, and social interactions.

But what happens when you're dressed as though it was tailored specifically for you? You're unstoppable, honey. Your energy changes, your mood improves, and all of a sudden, anything appears feasible. You're laughing and smiling more and generally exuding positivity. And those in your immediate vicinity? They also notice that. Your tribe is drawn to you by your vibe, and you draw all that positive energy back to yourself when you're feeling good about yourself.

AND LET US NOT OVERLOOK the days when you don't feel so hot. Perhaps you awoke on the incorrect side of the bed, or perhaps life is simply presenting you with unexpected turns. On certain days, it really does matter what you wear. Since fashion is about feeling good as much as it is about looking nice. It's about utilizing your wardrobe to elevate your confidence, alter your attitude, and make your day. Therefore, grab that attire that makes you feel like a queen when you're having a bad day. Put on whatever it is that gives you a sense of power—heels, a dress, lipstick. And observe how your entire day transforms.

The impact of color on perception and behavior

Yes, you should start focusing on color as it represents a whole new level of fashion psychology. Colors do more for you than merely make your clothes appear nice. They have power, meaning, and the ability to alter both your own and other people's perceptions of you.

STYLING SUCCESS : HOW TO BUILD A WARDROBE THAT REFLECTS YOUR AMBITIONS

Scarlet? You have power, girl. When you enter a room dressed in crimson, you command attention. It's audacious, self-assured, and attention-grabbing to proclaim, "Look at me, I'm here, and I'm not backing down." What's the best thing, then? People react to it. They perceive you as a confident individual who knows what she wants and isn't scared to pursue it.

AND THEN THERE IS THE dark. Ahh, black is elegant, timeless, and possessing a hint of mystery. Black is the hue of authority, elegance, and power. Wearing it says, "I'm sophisticated, I'm in charge, and I'm not here to play games." And what about black beauty? It is adaptable. It always looks great and can be dressed up or down. The thing about black, though, is that it can act as a shield. It's the hue you wear to hide things from prying eyes and to protect yourself. It is safe in addition to being robust.

Not to be overlooked is white. White is pure, clean, and fresh. It represents fresh starts, hope, and simplicity. However, white has its own force and conveys a message of openness, honesty, and readiness for whatever comes your way. It's daring because wearing it isn't always simple. It requires confidence because everything is visible and there are no shadowy areas or things to hide behind. White is elegant and courageous.

However, color has more to do with perceptions than that. It also has to do with your self-perception. Consider your feelings when wearing particular hues. In blue, do you feel at ease? Invigorated by yellow? rooted in the green? That is the operation of color psychology. It's affecting your energy, your attitude, and your overall vibe. And you can begin to take advantage of color if you start to pay attention to that.

Do you want to have more self-assurance? Make a red move. Do you need to de-stress before a major meeting? Select blue. Do you want to feel energized and prepared to face the day? White is your best option. Knowing what makes you feel good and what functions for you is crucial. Use this information to your advantage. Because, sweetie, you begin to play with power the moment you begin to work with color. And you're going to win that game.

Dressing for the role you want, not just the one you have

DON'T JUST DRESS FOR the role you have; dress for the part you want. You see, style is more than just where you are at any one time. It concerns your destination. It's about using your wardrobe to bring your aspirations, objectives, and future to life. Because you begin to believe it when you dress like you've already achieved success. And you create it when you have faith in it.

Let's say your current position isn't exactly what you'd like to be doing. Even though you may be in an entry-level role, your goal is still to work in the corner office. Perhaps you're working toward a broader goal even though you're in a field that's not quite what you want to be in. In any event, you already have a vision for the future; now is the moment to start acting as though you've arrived.

This does not imply that you have to spend your whole salary on high-end clothing (unless that's your thing; no judgment intended). It simply means that you should start considering how you want to feel and be perceived, and then choose your clothing accordingly. Start dressing like the boss if you want to be in charge. Wear items of clothing that give you a sense of empowerment, control, and accomplished arrival.

The worst part is that when you start dressing for the part you want to play, other people begin to perceive you as that role. People begin to regard you more seriously, assign you greater responsibilities, and perceive you as a person with potential. It's as like you're letting the universe and those in your immediate vicinity know that you're prepared for more and a step forward. And the cosmos will react, I promise you.

It goes beyond how other people perceive you, though. It has to do with your self-perception. You begin to feel like the woman you want to be when you dress like her. You begin to adopt a new mannerism, speak with greater power, and move more audaciously. That's also where the magic occurs. Because you begin to make it a reality when you have confidence in yourself and imagine yourself as that person already.

THEREFORE, DRESS APPROPRIATELY for the work you have. Wear what you would want to work. Wear what makes you feel like you're already living your dream, rather than just what is required of you. It's time for you to start utilizing fashion, sis, as a strong weapon to design the life you desire. Your wardrobe may help you achieve your goals, whether they involve starting your own business, getting that promotion, or simply moving up the social ladder. So take a step into the future, dress for success each time, and see how your life begins to transform.

Fashion is about more than just clothes. There is an entire vibe to it. It's a means of communicating your identity, feelings, and future goals. It's about projecting your dreams, elevating your attitude, and shaping your reality with color, style, and confidence. Furthermore, the influence of fashion becomes evident when you learn about the psychology behind it. Use it, then. Accept it. Most importantly, enjoy yourself while doing it. You can accomplish anything when you feel confident in your attire. And it is fashion's true power.

YES, THAT IS IT. AN honest discussion about the psychology of fashion. It's time to start dressing like a queen and utilizing fashion as your covert weapon.

Building a Style Vision Board

Don't limit your sense of style to wearing whatever you have in your closet. No, what matters is having purpose, being aware of your identity and destination, and dressed appropriately. However, how does one go from staring vacantly at their closet to walking down the runway like a pro? A style vision board can be useful in this situation. We are discussing the process of realizing your fashion aspirations, piece by piece. So let's get started on how to gather and organize your inspiration, transform it into a look that is uniquely yours, and establish some concrete objectives to make your closet seem as good as it can.

STYLING SUCCESS : HOW TO BUILD A WARDROBE THAT REFLECTS YOUR AMBITIONS

Collecting and curating fashion inspiration

Your vision board will serve as your guide if you're serious about raising the ante on your style game. However, you must first collect all of those tiny inspiration sparks that give you a heart palpitation. You know the ones: those ensembles that force you to pause your scrolling, those eye-catching hues, and those accessories that beg to be worn. All that good things needs to be gathered and claimed by you.

TAKE A DAILY DOSE OF scrolling first. Pinterest, TikTok, and Instagram are going to be your new best pals. But now you're scrolling with a goal; you're not just scrolling for fun. Keep things that speak to you close at hand. Make boards, folders, or whatever else you need to keep everything organized. Don't stop there, though. Everything is up for grabs, including magazines, billboards, and random fly girls you meet in the street. Make everything necessary to capture that inspiration—cut, screenshot, save. It's imperative that you become into a fashion sponge, absorbing all the gorgeous style that you come across.

Don't just grab everything now, please. Choose your spots, young lady. Curation, not collection, is the focus here. You want to collect items that seem like they belong in your story and that speak to you. Perhaps it's the edge of some fierce boots, the sophistication of a fitted blazer, or the boldness of a red lip. Make sure it speaks to you, whatever it is. If it doesn't make you say, "Oh my god, yes!"feel, it's not appropriate for your board.

Additionally, remember the vibes, sweetheart. Fashion is much more than simply clothes; it's about the vibe they convey. Are you attracted to a boss in a sharp suit because of their confidence and power? Or perhaps the easygoing, carefree air of someone who appears to have just left a Bali beach? Seize the moment, whatever it may be, and include it into your board. A collection of pictures, hues, textures, and other elements that collectively convey the narrative of who you are or who you are becoming is what you desire.

Translating your vision into a cohesive style plan

It's time to put all that inspiration to use now that you have it all in one location. Now is the moment to turn your vision into a style plan that will get you from your current situation to your ideal one. Hold on, this isn't about emulating other people's styles. No, it's about embracing your passions and making them uniquely your own. Identifying the links among all those components and developing your own distinctive style language are key.

Start by observing trends. Which hues are more prevalent? Do particular materials or silhouettes appeal to you? Perhaps you're all about the minimalist look or you have a thing for large prints. Start identifying the themes, whatever they may be, and see how they connect. This is the point at which your idea begins to take form. You're witnessing the emergence of a distinct style that is uniquely you, not just a collection of aimless outfits.

NEXT, CONSIDER YOUR way of life. Your life should not fit your clothing, but your life should fit your clothes. Your wardrobe will appear different for someone who is all about the freelancing, creative life than it will for someone who is a boss chick working in the corporate sector. Nevertheless, your style must blend in with whatever your life may seem like. No matter where you are or what you're doing, you want to feel at ease and like yourself. So have it in mind when you're creating your plan. How can you use all that creativity to create a wardrobe that suits your everyday routine?

THE BOTTOM LINE IS that you need to ensure that your whole look is well-coordinated. This indicates that everything is compatible,

STYLING SUCCESS : HOW TO BUILD A WARDROBE THAT REFLECTS YOUR AMBITIONS

allowing you to mix and match like an expert. Your goal is to assemble a wardrobe in which each item complements the others. In this manner, you won't be left with a closet full of items that don't match together. Consider the larger picture. Does that statement jacket go well with anything else in your closet? Is it possible to pair those striking shoes with multiple outfits? If not, perhaps it's time to reconsider.

Setting wardrobe goals that align with your ambitions

It's time to establish some goals now that your vision is beginning to take shape. Not just any objectives, but wardrobe goals that complement your aspirations are what I mean. Because dressed like the woman you want to be is just as important as looking attractive when it comes to fashion. And it entails establishing objectives that move you closer to your vision.

Begin by determining your desired destination after six months, a year, or five years. What is the dream about? Is there something wrong in the boardroom? Being a business owner yourself? Exploring the globe in elegance? Whatever it is, you should dress accordingly. You start to believe it's doable when you dress as though you've already achieved success. So, make sure your wardrobe goals are in line with your lofty aspirations. Purchasing a few essential items that give you a boss-like feeling could be the solution. Perhaps it's designing a capsule wardrobe that simplifies packing for trips that take you across the world. Make sure that whatever it is, is bringing you closer to your desired destination.

Set wise goals instead than just any old goals. To maintain that momentum, you want to make sure they are doable. Divide them into manageable steps. Perhaps you should start by organizing your closet and getting rid of anything that doesn't go with your plan. After then, it's about gradually expanding your wardrobe. everything's not necessary to finish everything all at once. The components that will give you the best value for your money are the necessities, so start there.

Then, add those focal pieces—the ones that truly make your vision come to life—gradually.

Additionally, remember to take care of yourself. Are you achieving your objectives? Is the lady you want to be beginning to appear in your clothes? It's time to make adjustments if not. Perhaps you have a clearer view now, or you have recognized something isn't functioning properly. It's alright, dear. Style is not a destination; it is a progression. Continue making adjustments, honing your craft, and challenging yourself to dress like the lady you know you are.

THAT'S ALL THERE IS to it, lady. Creating a style vision board is more than just sticking lovely images on the wall; it's about mapping out your future self. It involves gathering inspiration, turning it into a strategy, and establishing objectives that are consistent with your aspirations. Above all, it's about enjoying yourself while doing it. Wearing clothing should make you happy and give you the opportunity to live the life you desire. Now grab those scissors and go to work cutting, pinning, and creating the wardrobe that will help you achieve your goals. You can do anything you set your mind to when you dress intentionally and like the lady you want to be. You can do this, girl. Go ahead and kill it.

It's time to get to work now that you know the ins and outs of creating a style vision board. Begin gathering, organizing, arranging, and establishing objectives. Your style, aspirations, and dreams should all be reflected in your outfit. And never forget, my dear, that true fashion is about feeling wonderful on the inside as much as the outside. Thus, develop the wardrobe that will propel you to the top while being imaginative and having fun. It's time for the rest of the world to realize that you deserve nothing less than the best. Show them what you're made of, go ahead.

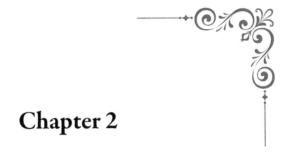

Chapter 2

The Essential Wardrobe Foundation

Must-Have Basics for Every Wardrobe

A strong foundation is necessary to create a house, and the same is true for your closet. The essentials are what you need since they will support you through everything. When you're staring at your closet as if it owes you something, we're talking about classic pieces that never go out of style and always have your back. However, having the appropriate items isn't enough; you also need to know what to look for, why quality is more important than quantity, and how to spend money on wardrobe essentials that are both fashionable and functional.

STYLING SUCCESS : HOW TO BUILD A WARDROBE THAT REFLECTS YOUR AMBITIONS

Timeless pieces that never go out of style

We're talking about those ride-or-die things that never fail, no matter the situation, when it comes to essential necessities. These are the classic pieces that are always in style and will be worn frequently regardless of what the newest trends are. You need these in your life, I promise.

Now, I'm not talking about any old white shirt here; rather, I'm referring to that elegant, expertly tailored one that gives you the impression that you're in control of your life, even when you're not. Girl, this shirt is so versatile. With just a few accessory changes, you can transition from a corporate meeting to brunch with your girlfriends. You may tie it up, tuck it in, button it up, or leave it half-open. The options are unlimited. It's fresh, clean, and reliable every time.

The tiny black dress is the next item on the list. You're playing yourself, sis, if you don't have one of them in your closet. Your best tool, your hidden weapon, is the LBD. It's the one dress that's always up to the task, be it an unexpected party invitation, a work function, or a heated date. Even when you're simply winging it, you always look like you know precisely what you're doing because to its sleek, elegant design.

NOT A DISCUSSION ABOUT classic clothes would be complete without including a well-fitting pair of jeans. Not just any jeans, though, listen. You need that pair that accentuates your butt, gives you the perfect amount of support, and gives you confidence to take on the world. It doesn't matter if the jeans are black, medium wash, or dark wash as long as they fit you like a glove. You're going to wear these jeans everywhere—from casual Fridays to running errands to meeting up for coffee with that hot gym bunny.

The timeless blazer is another essential. I know some of you think blazers are only appropriate for the workplace, but let me tell you, they're also a powerful style statement. A well-fitting blazer can quickly transform any ensemble from "cute" to "queen." Wear it over a dress to provide structure, or pair it with jeans for a more carefree style. Your secret weapon, girl, is the blazer; it puts everything together and gives you a polished appearance even when you're anything but.

Not to be overlooked is a great pair of black pumps. You recognize the ones: stylish, modest, and sleek. These shoes will always lead you in the right direction. Even while you're strutting down the street, they may make you feel like you're walking on air and go with everything. You need that one pair that is both fierce and statement-making, yet comfortable enough to wear all day. Unquestionably, black pumps are a wardrobe staple.

Quality Is More Important Than Quantity

I understand how alluring it may be to stock your closet with the newest styles, especially with quick fashion making it so simple. Let me tell you something, though: sometimes less is more. Having a small selection of high-quality pieces that make you feel like a million bucks is preferable to having a closet full of inexpensive items that rip apart quickly.

INVESTING IN QUALITY is an investment in oneself. You're claiming that you're worthy. nice clothing is built to last. I should have clothes that fit well, feel nice, and last beyond a season. They don't lose their shape after washing, they don't fade, and you won't feel like a bad shopper. And let's face it, you feel different when you're dressed with quality. You feel like you've got everything together, walk a little more confidently, and raise your head a little.

THE TRUTH IS, THOUGH, that price does not always equate to quality. It entails being meticulous with the details. Examine the sewing, touch the material, and ensure that it fits. A well-made article of apparel ought to feel substantial and long-lasting. It should embrace you in all the right places and give you room to breathe where you need it to, fitting you like it was made especially for you. Above all, it ought to make you feel good.

Not to be overlooked is the cost per wear consideration. Over time, quality investments result in financial savings. That jacket you invested a bit more money in? It will last for years on you. The jeans that fit perfectly? After a few washings, they won't sag or lose their shape. Well-made items endure, so you won't need to replace them as often. And that's how you create a wardrobe that will last, sis.

How to invest in versatile staples

These are the pieces that will carry the most weight in your wardrobe—they are adaptable enough to be dressed up or down and used in countless combinations. Versatility is essential while making investments in basics. You want outfits that are versatile enough to carry you from work to play, from the office to the weekend, without sacrificing style.

It's important to start with the foundation. After discussing the essential elements that will never go out of style, it's time to consider how they will complement one another. Consider the big picture when you're out buying basics. How does this item match the rest of your wardrobe? Is it suitable for a variety of outfits? Is it possible to style it for various events? It is worth the investment if the response is in the affirmative.

Take that timeless white shirt, for instance. It can accomplish everything, which makes it a staple. For a sophisticated business style, tuck it into a pencil skirt. Alternatively, tie it at the waist and wear it with high-waisted jeans for a laid-back weekend approach. Wear it alone in the summer or layered with a sweater in the winter. That's the specific type of adaptability you seek. You want items that you can style differently for every occasion, every season, and every situation.

An excellent pair of black pants is equivalent. Black pants, whether they are slim-fit jeans or tailored pants, are a wardrobe essential since they complement everything. For a more casual approach, pair them with sneakers and a graphic tee, or wear them with a jacket and pumps for a more professional appearance. For a night out, you could even dress them up with a silk top and striking jewelry. You can draw anything you want on a blank canvas, which is what black jeans are like.

An excellent leather jacket is another multipurpose need. Although this one may seem a little more specialized, a quality leather jacket can really make a big difference in your clothing. It's the ideal topping for jeans and a t-shirt, it provides a sophisticated outfit some attitude, and it gives a floral dress some edge. Furthermore, it gets better with age. One item that is well worth the investment is a leather jacket because it gets better with each wear.

MOREOVER, PAY ATTENTION to accessories, sis. Any ensemble may be made more stylish with a striking necklace, a well-made handbag, or a timeless pair of sunglasses. These are the elements that give your wardrobe character and make it distinctively yours. Don't overlook the finishing touches while purchasing essentials. A well-chosen item can elevate an otherwise ordinary ensemble.

There you have it: the essential pieces that every wardrobe should own. These are the things that will support you no matter what and will serve as the cornerstone of your style. Having the appropriate components is important, but so is understanding their significance and how to make wise investments in them. Investing in quality over quantity and versatility over trends is the key to creating a wardrobe that suits your current style and future aspirations. Go ahead, sis, and begin laying that foundation. Your clothes will thank you, as will your self-assurance.

RECALL THAT INVESTING in quality, selecting adaptability above fads, and owning the correct pieces that fit you are the keys to building a strong wardrobe foundation. Instead than just being a collection of items, your wardrobe should represent your goals and sense of style. Thus, begin with the fundamentals, build upon them, and see how your style changes as you do. When everything is in place, dressing doesn't only mean looking nice; it also means feeling unstoppable. And you are unstoppable, sis—trust me.

Building a Capsule Wardrobe

Now, I realize that sophisticated stylists and fashion bloggers have undoubtedly used this term before, but let me to explain it to you in a way that makes sense. Putting together a set of items that you genuinely enjoy wearing, that go well together, and that simplify your life is the foundation of a capsule wardrobe. We're not here to wow people with an endless collection of things we never wear. No, ma'am. We live for the kind of life when getting dressed in the morning is effortless and every item has a purpose.

Creating a functional and flexible wardrobe

First things first: we're going to design a versatile and useful wardrobe. One that doesn't simply work for the gram, but one that genuinely works for your life. Let's be honest: it's simple to get sucked into the hoopla surrounding trends and what other people are wearing. You should service your clothes, not the other way around.

Consider your daily routine when creating your capsule clothing. What is it that you really need? You need components that can keep up if you're rushing to meetings, picking up the kids, and going out to dinner with friends all in the same day. You should wear clothing that is easy to mix and match, comfy, and versatile. We're talking about outfits that look amazing even when you can toss them on carelessly.

THE CORNERSTONE OF your capsule wardrobe is your fundamentals. Start there. These are the components that will hold everything else in place. Consider a few well-fitting jeans, timeless t-shirts, a short black dress, and a dapper blazer. Wearing these outfits will take you anyplace. You only need to choose the best possibilities; you don't need a hundred. the items that, each time you wear them, make you feel fantastic. The secret to a functional wardrobe is having items that work with you rather than against you.

STYLING SUCCESS : HOW TO BUILD A WARDROBE THAT REFLECTS YOUR AMBITIONS

The truth is that you also require flexibility. Your clothing should be able to transition with you when the seasons, occasions, and emotions change. Therefore, don't forget to incorporate a few statement pieces that express your individuality while you're concentrating on your basics. A unique printed dress, a coat in a striking color, or a killer pair of heels. Your basics go from being "cute" to "I'm here, and I'm killing it" with these components.

AND AVOID GETTING CAUGHT up in the idea that this requires you to buy a complete new outfit. Sometimes all you need to do is organize the things you already own. Take a peek at your wardrobe and consider what items you use frequently. Which ones give me the most sense of who I am? These are the parts of your capsule. The remainder? Perhaps it's time for them to go. Not tension, but delight should come from your closet.

Mixing and matching to maximize outfit options

The allure of a capsule wardrobe lies in its ability to be versatile. You should choose items that you can style differently, wear in different ways, and change up according to your mood. Here's where your inventiveness becomes useful. Play around with your wardrobe, try different looks, and venture outside of your comfort zone without fear.

Let's begin with something basic: your go-to pair of pants. Though you've worn them a million times with sneakers and a t-shirt, how about dressing them up with heels and a silk blouse? Or perhaps dressing cozy for fall by donning boots and a bulky sweater? In the summer, the same jeans look great worn casually with a tank top and sandals. When you're willing to try new things, the possibilities are virtually limitless.

FURTHERMORE, IT GOES beyond just tops and bottoms. Your best friend when it comes to mixing and matching are accessories. A simple black dress can look completely different depending on how you style it. Pair it with a denim jacket and flats for a daytime look, then switch to a statement necklace and heels for a night out. Or maybe throw on a wide-brimmed hat and ankle boots for something a little edgier. It's all about taking what you have and making it work in new ways.

Another way to boost your clothing possibilities is layering. This is where you can really get creative, especially when the seasons change. Take the same dress and layer it over a turtleneck in the winter, or under a long cardigan in the fall. Add tights, scarves, belts—whatever feels appropriate. Layering provides your wardrobe so much more mileage because it allows you to wear the same pieces in multiple ways, depending on the weather and the occasion.

And don't sleep on color, sis. A burst of color can take a plain look to the next level. If you've got a lot of neutral staples in your capsule wardrobe, add a few bright accessories to spice things up. A vibrant scarf, a striking handbag, or even a statement shoe may shift the whole tone of your ensemble. The idea is to have fun with it and not be hesitant to try something new.

Remember, the idea here is to make your clothing work for you. You don't need a wardrobe full of clothing to have a ton of outfit alternatives. You only need to know how to mix and match what you've got. And when you do that, sis, you'll never feel like you have nothing to wear again.

Seasonal adjustments and layering techniques

Alright, now let's speak about seasonal changes and layering approaches. Because let's be honest—weather may be unpredictable, and your wardrobe needs to be able to roll with the punches. But fear not, lady—you can maintain the effectiveness of your capsule wardrobe throughout the year with a few well-chosen pieces.

The seasons don't require you to buy new clothes for every look. It all comes down to making little changes that will keep you fashionable and comfortable regardless of the weather. Having a few essential transitional pieces in your closet is the first step. These are the pieces that you can layer up in the winter or wear alone in the summer.

Once you get the hang of it, girl, you'll question how you ever got along without it. The goal of layering is to keep warm while enhancing the depth and dimension of your ensemble. It's also a fantastic method to keep your summer clothing going into the fall and winter.

As the layer that will be closest to your skin, start with your base layer. Something airy and light, like a thin turtleneck or tank top, is what it should be. You can then begin to contribute to it. A jacket over your shirt, a sweater over your turtleneck, or a button-up shirt over your tank top. You may take off or put back on layers as needed during the day, and each one adds warmth and style.

Remember to include outerwear as well. When the weather gets colder, a nice coat is necessary, but it doesn't have to be plain. Seek out coats that give your ensemble a distinguishing touch, such as a striking hue, an intriguing texture, or a distinctive shape. Depending on your taste and the weather where you reside, a trench coat, wool coat, or puffer jacket can all be excellent choices.

When it comes to layering, scarves, hats, and gloves are also your greatest friends. They're not only useful, but they're also a simple way to give your ensemble some flair. A basic sweater and trousers may be elevated to a whole new level with a thick knit scarf. Not to be overlooked are boots. Even when it's snowing outside, a beautiful pair of boots may give you the confidence to take on the world.

Consider fabrics as well while making seasonal modifications. Lightweight, breathable materials like cotton and linen are ideal for the summer. However, you should transition to thicker materials like fleece, cashmere, and wool during the winter. If you take care of these materials, they will keep you warm without adding bulk and last you for many years.

HERE'S A LITTLE ADVICE: don't be scared to switch out items for different seasons. That summer dress of yours that you adore? In the fall, dress it as a skirt by throwing on a sweater over it. The summertime shorts you looked so good in? For a stylish winter look, pair them with tights and boots. With a little imagination, your wardrobe can fit you all year round and not just be a one-season wonder.

And there you have it. Creating a capsule wardrobe is about having better rather than just less. It's about building an outfit collection that suits you, makes getting ready simple, and ensures that you always look and feel amazing. Focusing on quality, adaptability, and layering makes your wardrobe an effective tool that supports you in becoming your best self every day.

STYLING SUCCESS : HOW TO BUILD A WARDROBE THAT REFLECTS YOUR AMBITIONS

ULTIMATELY, YOUR CLOTHING should represent who you are—sturdy, adaptable, and prepared for anything. So go ahead, sis, and start putting together that capsule outfit. Your future self will be appreciative.

AND NEVER FORGET, LADY, that the whole point of fashion is to convey your identity and direction. The idea behind a capsule wardrobe is to give you the flexibility to be who you really are, no matter what obstacles life throws at you. It is not about restricting yourself. Now go out there and layer up like the queen you are, rock those classic pieces, and mix and match with assurance. This is something you can handle.

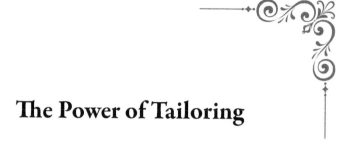

The Power of Tailoring

It's time to wake up if you have been sleeping on the strength of a good fit. The key to appearing like a million dollars, no matter where you shop or what you wear, is tailoring. Even with the most exquisite clothing, it won't benefit you if it doesn't fit properly. Now, let's discuss the importance of fit, how to choose a reliable tailor, and how to give tailoring first priority when on a tight budget. Because your entire sense of style will elevate once you realize the power of tailoring, I promise.

Why fit is everything

Fit is crucial. Clearly. Even if you purchase the most costly designer item, it won't look good if it hangs off your shoulders or squeezes you in the wrong places. Conversely, you may make a $20 dress from the discount rack appear custom-made by making the appropriate adjustments. That is how customization works.

Your best features are accentuated and you exude confidence when your clothes fit you flawlessly. It's all about confidence, my dear. The world notices when you walk and talk differently because you know you look beautiful. This is the reason fit is so crucial. It's not only about the clothes; it's also about your emotional connection to them.

DON'T GET ME WRONG, fit does not imply that everything must be incredibly tight. That means your wardrobe should complement your figure, not contradict it. Regardless of your body type—thin, tall, curvaceous, or anywhere in between—your clothing should fit you well and make you feel your best. The truth is that not every item you purchase off the rack will fit you flawlessly right out of the box. That is the use of tailoring.

You can alter your garments to fit your particular body form using tailoring. Have big hips but a petite waist? A skilled tailor knows how to trim that waist while leaving room for the hips. A short torso but long legs? No worries, your tops and pants can be adjusted by a tailor to make everything look proportionate. Making your clothes work for you rather than the other way around is the core of tailoring.

YOU ARE LOSING OUT, if you have never had a suit custom-fitted to your exact measurements. You can feel strong, put together, and ready to take on the world when you wear a well-fitting suit. It's well worth the money and is comparable to armor for today's women.

Finding and working with a good tailor

Because not all tailors are made equal and you want someone with experience in the field.

Ask around first things first. The greatest method to locate an excellent tailor is by word of mouth. Find out from your loved ones where they get their clothes altered, or even ask that fashionable coworker. You would be shocked at how many people have a favorite and trusted tailor. After receiving a few recommendations, further investigate. Examine internet evaluations, go to the store, and inquire about the experience. Make sure they are knowledgeable, competent, and know what you're searching for.

Start with something basic, like hems, waist adjustments, or taking in a top, after you've found a tailor you like. You will be able to observe their work and how they handle your clothing as a result. You can start entrusting them with more intricate adjustments, such as jackets, dresses, or suits, if they perform well.

ALSO, DON'T BE SHY about speaking up. Working with a tailor requires open communication. Make sure your goals are clear, and don't be hesitant to ask questions. They are the expert, after all, so ask them if you have any questions. Ultimately, it's your body and your clothes, so don't settle for anything less than ideal.

DEVELOPING A RELATIONSHIP with your tailor is also a smart move. They'll be able to customize your clothes more effectively the more they get to know you and your style. And believe me when I say that a good tailor is worth their weight in gold once you discover one. A skilled tailor can elevate your wardrobe to a new level by making each item appear custom-made for you.

Tailoring on a budget: What to prioritize

I understand your thought process—tailoring may seem wonderful, but the cost might be high. You're true, my dear; while tailoring isn't always inexpensive, it is an investment in your clothing and yourself. Nevertheless, there are ways to prioritize what is personalized and what isn't if you're on a tight budget.

Start by concentrating on your most worn items. These are the most well-worn items of clothing that you wear every day. Since you'll be getting your money's worth, it's worth investing a little bit more to ensure that these pieces suit you precisely. If you wear jeans every day, for instance, ensure sure they are custom-fit to your exact measurements. Alternatively, if you have a favorite jacket that you wear to work, consider having it altered to fit you perfectly.

NEXT, ORDER THE COMPONENTS that you invested in. These are the classic, well-made pieces in your wardrobe that you want to hold onto for a long time. Imagine that power suit, that little black dress, or that timeless trench coat. Since they will not go out of style anytime

STYLING SUCCESS : HOW TO BUILD A WARDROBE THAT REFLECTS YOUR AMBITIONS

soon and you want them to fit you perfectly for years to come, these are the pieces that are worth tailoring.

IT'S ALSO WORTHWHILE to have your clothing customized if you have an upcoming special occasion. You want to appear your best for any event—a wedding, a job interview, or a big presentation—and tailoring may make all the difference. A well-fitting dress or suit might provide you with the extra self-assurance you require to shine.

What about the items for which you are unsure whether customizing them is worthwhile? Here's a tiny tip: try them on and observe your feelings. Take it to your tailor to see what they can do if the garment is perfect for you but the fit isn't quite right. However, it could be time to let it go if you're not in love with it. Although tailoring can do wonders, it won't make a piece of clothing that you dislike into something you adore. Let your tailor perform their magic on the clothing that truly make you feel fantastic. Keep your focus on those.

Here's another piece of advice: don't overlook thrift and secondhand stores. Some excellent items may be found for a much lower price, and with some minor tailoring, they can appear really expensive. Thus, if you're on a tight budget, check out your neighborhood thrift stores to uncover such treasures, then take them to your tailor for a personalized fit. It's an excellent approach to assemble a fashionable, fine-quality wardrobe without going over budget.

Finally, don't be hesitant to consult your tailor about what items are worth modifying and which ones are not. If an item is worth the investment, a professional tailor will tell you the truth. If money is tight, they can also provide alternatives, such as little tweaks that can have a significant impact without breaking the bank

There you have it, sis—the power of customization. The key is to locate a competent tailor who can make your style come to life, invest in things that make you feel like your best self, and make your clothes work for you. Anyone who wants to feel and look their best can benefit from tailoring; it's not just for the wealthy and famous. Therefore, don't be scared to go the extra mile and get your clothing made to fit you exactly. You feel good when your clothing fit you, and when you feel good, there's nothing you can't accomplish.

AND NEVER FORGET THAT the whole point of fashion, sis, is to show who you are. Adding tailoring to your arsenal of style tools can help you project an image of yourself that is strong, self-assured, and prepared to take on the world. So go ahead, make an investment in yourself and leave the magic to your tailor. Every day, you should feel and look your best.

Chapter 3

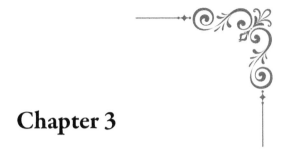

Dressing for Success in the Workplace

Understanding Dress Codes

I understand your thought process now: "Do I really have to adhere to all of these dress codes?" But trust me when I say that negotiating dress standards is much more than just following the rules—it's about knowing how to use the situation to your advantage. In the business environment, your appearance can have a significant impact on how people see you, how you conduct yourself, and how you are handled. Let's break it down: knowing business casual, creative, and corporate settings; modifying your wardrobe for various work contexts; and dressing for responsibilities particular to your industry.

Navigating corporate, business casual, and creative environments

The first thing you need to know about the kind of setting you're entering is whether you're starting a new job or wanting to improve your style at your existing one. This is a multi-level thing, sis. Each type of setting—creative, corporate, and business casual—has a distinct atmosphere that you must know how to pull off.

First, let's discuss **corporations**. This is the land of suits and no nonsense, where everything is perfectly in place. Recall those meetings in boardrooms where everyone is dressed in formal attire, dark hues, and straight lines. It's all about power dressing in this setting. Your clothes should convey a sense of professionalism while maintaining your individuality. This entails form-fitting blazers, precisely designed pants or pencil skirts, and sophisticated dresses that fall just perfectly. Your go-to colors should be neutrals like black, navy, and gray, but don't be scared to add a burst of color with an accessory or shirt. And footwear? Keep them elegant, dear. Nothing too loud, either polished flats or heels. The goal is to be respected without drawing attention away from the task at hand.

Business casual is the next outfit to wear. This one is a little trickier because it allows for a little more leeway, but that doesn't mean you can take it easy. The key to business casual style is balance: you want to seem polished without coming off as rigid. It's the medium ground where you can remain professional but exhibit a little more personality. You can mix and match in this situation by wearing a pencil skirt with a looser-fitting shirt or a jacket with pants. You can experiment further with colors and patterns, but maintain a clean look. Remember, this is still work and not a fashion display, even with a statement piece like a colorful necklace or a printed scarf. And footwear? Ankle boots, loafers, or chic flats look wonderful in this setting. Style meets comfort, my dear. That's what the game is all about.

STYLING SUCCESS : HOW TO BUILD A WARDROBE THAT REFLECTS YOUR AMBITIONS

Let's now enter the creative setting. This is your chance to truly show off your inner fashionista. Consider sectors such as design, media, and advertising, where uniqueness is valued and promoted. Here, you may express your originality through your wardrobe, so go ahead and try new things. You can combine formal and informal, retro and contemporary, and high and low. It all comes down to expression. Perhaps you wear bright prints with your best denim or a wacky graphic tee with a fitted blazer. Add-ons? Go berserk. This is the place to wear bold bags, quirky eyewear, and earrings that make a statement. However, and this is crucial, you still need to pay attention to the environment. It doesn't necessarily make sense to do anything creatively. Recognize when something is too casual and when it is fashionable. Sis, you want to make a lasting impression—not by appearing in anything that casts doubt on your judgment.

Modifying Your Look for Various Work Environments

Now that you understand the many kinds of work environments, what happens if you have to juggle more than one? Perhaps you have a business meeting in the morning and a networking event in the evening, or perhaps you are relocating from a corporate office to a creative studio on the same day. Being adaptable is essential to navigating these shifts, sis. You need clothing in your closet that can change with the circumstances you find yourself in.

Let's imagine you have a business meeting in the morning and a more laid-back client lunch in the afternoon. Start with an outfit that screams business: a smart blazer, fitted pants, and a timeless top. You could now wear a leather jacket or a looser-fitting cardigan instead of the blazer for that lunch, and you'll be set. Alternatively, perhaps you have an event at a more imaginative location after work and a day at the office. Start with something business casual in this situation, such a classy dress that is appropriate for the workplace but still fashionable. For the evening function, swap up your workplace blazer for a statement piece of jewellery and a fierce pair of heels.

HAVING EFFORTLESSLY transitional pieces in your wardrobe is the goal. Here, your best friends are dresses with lots of wearability, cardigans, and blazers. You should be able to change up your appearance while maintaining a polished appearance with the least amount of work. Additionally, don't overlook your bag. A well-sized, fashionable purse that can accommodate all of your daily necessities, along with additional shoes or accessories, is an invaluable possession.

IT'S ALSO IMPORTANT to consider the function of accessories. The simplest method to change the look of your outfit is with accessories. Maybe you're wearing a basic dress, but when you

STYLING SUCCESS : HOW TO BUILD A WARDROBE THAT REFLECTS YOUR AMBITIONS

accessorize it with a bright necklace and earrings, it becomes appropriate for a more creative setting. Alternatively, you may just be wearing a simple blazer and pants; change your work bag for a clutch and add some interesting shoes, and you're set for a great night out. It's all about the small things that can transform your appearance from formal to informal, standard to remarkable, and day to night.

Dressing appropriately for industry-specific roles

LET'S GET DOWN TO BUSINESS and discuss how to dress for your particular career. Since what is effective in one field may be wholly inappropriate in another, let's confront it. Additionally, you need to look the part if you want to succeed.

Let us begin with the business world, which includes the fields of banking, law, and consulting, all of which have high stakes and even higher demands. You're working with people's money, legal issues, and business plans in these industries, so you better believe that they expect you to always present yourself in a polished and professional manner. This calls for dressing appropriately. The standard is tailored suits, dapper button-downs, and timeless loafers or pumps. Opt for muted hues like black, gray, or navy as they communicate dependability and authority. Additionally, make sure your clothing is well-fitting, clean, and pressed at all times. This is not the place to push the boundaries or try new trends. The first step in projecting expertise and confidence is how you dress.

Conversely, in the creative professions of fashion, media, and entertainment, your personal style can hold equal significance to your portfolio. There is more space for self-expression and much laxer rules here. Don't get me wrong, though: just because you can dress more casually or avant-gardely doesn't mean you should relax. Make your attire count because it can be the first thing that draws someone's attention. Think creatively by layering various textures, experimenting with colors, and combining prints. But always maintain a deliberate and professional style. You dress to encourage confidence in your creative abilities, not simply for yourself. And never forget that expectations still exist, even in the creative industries. Recognize your target, as well as the atmosphere of the workspace and dress appropriately.

Although pragmatism is the main focus in the healthcare and education industries, you may still add some elegance to your work. Even though healthcare workers frequently have to wear scrubs or uniforms, you may still personalize it. Perhaps it's a colorful undershirt or a quirky pair of sneakers. Small gestures that maintain your sense of self while remaining practical and businesslike. Being personable and at ease while maintaining professionalism is crucial in the teaching profession, particularly when working with children. Consider dressing comfortably yet stylishly, such as with dresses that have pockets, elegant cardigans, and all-day flats.

If you work in technology, you most likely work in one of the most informal sectors of the economy. In Silicon Valley, hoodies and jeans are practically required, but that doesn't mean you have to fit in. Making a small impression is beneficial, even in a relaxed setting. Perhaps underneath that hoodie is a fantastic graphic top or a stylish pair of sneakers that convey your style sense. The goal is to convey that you understand the culture while maintaining your unique perspective.

The hospitality sector includes hotels, restaurants, and event planning, where appearance is frequently a determining factor in employment. Here, the impression you give people has a direct bearing on how you seem. In a posh restaurant or hotel, this entails dressing professionally, tastefully, and personably. Consider timeless silhouettes, immaculate footwear, and opulent accessories. Even though you might need to dress more frugally when organizing events, you can still seem fashionable. A stylish yet practical dress, some eye-catching accessories, and comfy shoes will all help you look great.

STYLING SUCCESS : HOW TO BUILD A WARDROBE THAT REFLECTS YOUR AMBITIONS

Whatever your industry, it's important to know what's expected of you and to dress appropriately. However, remember to add a little bit of your own individuality to the mixture. Fashion, after all, is about expressing who you are, even at work, sis. Recognize the guidelines, but don't be scared.

Power Dressing

Clothes that Command Respect

Pay attention, lady. If there's one thing that successful people in the business world need to understand, it's that power dressing is more than just looking nice; it's about taking charge of your image, commanding respect, and let your clothing speak for you. Have you ever entered a room and felt like everyone is staring at you—not because you're the loudest person, but rather because you exude confidence? That is the influence of well-tailored clothing. And I can assure you that it will completely transform your career.

STYLING SUCCESS : HOW TO BUILD A WARDROBE THAT REFLECTS YOUR AMBITIONS

The Effect of Professional Image-Building Clothes

Even if you are the most skilled, knowledgeable, and proficient in your field, if you appear disheveled and unprofessional when you enter a room, guess what? You won't be taken seriously by anyone. Brutal? Perhaps.

However, that is the truth. Even before you talk, the way you dress conveys a lot. It functions as a nonverbal introduction that establishes your impression, much like your personal brand statement.

Now, I'm not arguing that in order to be taken seriously, you have to spend a fortune or wear the newest styles. That is not the point. Making thoughtful decisions that represent who you are and where you want to go is key. People should be able to see by your wardrobe that you are here to lead, take initiative, and alter the course of events rather than just take part.

CONSIDER THIS: WHEN you dress nicely, you walk and talk differently, and your thoughts are also altered. With your shoulders back and your head held higher, you're prepared to take on any challenge that comes your way. That is the result of wearing power attire. It's more than simply your wardrobe; it's also about the attitude you give off when you think you look well. It's about showing up to that client meeting, networking event, or boardroom and taking charge of every minute of it.

TO BE CLEAR, FEELING good about yourself is more important than pleasing other people, though that is undoubtedly a factor. You perform better when you're dressed in a way that gives you a sense of strength. You're more self-assured, outspoken, and risk-taking. That is the influence of respect-demanding attire.

Critical Elements for Displaying Competence and Authority

So, what precisely should you wear to convey competence and authority? There is no one-size-fits-all approach to power dressing, so let's break it down. While it's important to identify what works for you, there are a few essential components that are always going to change the game.

Now for the blazer. Honey, you're missing out on great style if your closet doesn't have at least one go-to blazer. In business, a well-fitting blazer is equivalent to a suit of armor. It makes anything you're wearing seem instantly better because it's sharp and structured. A blazer is that item that shouts, "I'm in charge," whether it's worn over a dress, with fitted pants, or even with jeans for a more laid-back vibe. Additionally, don't be afraid to experiment with color; while conventional hues like black, navy, and gray will always work, a striking color can really help you stand out.

LET'S MOVE ON TO THE topic of fitted pants. I'm not referring to those formless, sagging pants that make no difference to your physique. I'm referring to pants that fit you like they were custom-made. Whether you choose a thin, wide-legged, or high-waisted cut, the fit is crucial. You may look polished and professional while still looking stylish with pants that are tailored to fit you. Additionally, they look great with almost anything, such as a stylish blouse or a clean button-down shirt.

WHEN IT COMES TO BUTTON-down shirts, every woman's closet should have a few of these. They don't have to be dull, either. A classic is a clean white button-down, but feel free to experiment with different materials, patterns, and hues. A silk button-down can give an air of sophistication, and a statement design lets you express your individuality without sacrificing style.

STYLING SUCCESS : HOW TO BUILD A WARDROBE THAT REFLECTS YOUR AMBITIONS

One of the secret weapons in the power dressing toolbox is the dress. When worn properly, they are comfortable, adaptable, and have the potential to be very strong. The silhouette is crucial; it should accentuate your best features without being overtly revealing. Consider A-line, sheath, and wrap styles for dresses. Wearing it with heels creates a look that is extremely powerful, polished, and feminine.

NOT TO BE OVERLOOKED are shoes. You can make or ruin an outfit with your shoes, sis. Elevate your look with a pair of well-heeled shoes to add even more confidence. Whether you choose elegant loafers, fashionable ankle boots, or traditional pumps, your shoes should be both comfortable to walk in and fashionable enough to draw attention. And please, look after your shoes! Nothing destroys an outfit more quickly than worn-out, scuffed shoes.

And last, add-ons. Now, you don't want to go overboard, but the appropriate accessories may truly complete an outfit. A striking watch, a statement jewelry, or even a structured handbag can provide the final touch to elevate your ensemble from decent to amazing. Just keep in mind that less is more—select one or two essential pieces that enhance your style without taking center stage.

WORKPLACE STYLE AND Practicality Balancing

It's great that power dressing is being discussed, but what about real life applications? Sis, if you're going to be hobbling around the workplace in a pencil skirt and 6-inch heels by midday or feeling out of breath at the end of the day, then you can't be wearing those outfits. Power dressing is about being able to perform at your best and feeling good, not just about looking nice.

Then, how can one strike a balance between fashion and utility? First, you need to be aware of your surroundings. Shoes that are both fashionable and comfy are essential if your job requires you to be on your feet for extended periods of time. That may include choosing more modest heels, sophisticated flats, or, if permitted by your employer, a chic pair of sneakers. Furthermore, don't assume that elegance must be sacrificed in favor of comfort. Many shoe brands are available that do both.

When it comes to clothing, fabric is everything. Select materials that are flexible, allow for air circulation, and resist wrinkling as soon as you sit down. Stretch textiles, cotton blends, and wool mixes are excellent choices for this. They maintain their form, are cozy, and have a polished appearance all day.

ADDING LAYERS IS ANOTHER piece of advice. Layers are a useful and stylish method to give your ensemble dimension. In a chilly office, you can stay warm with a blazer over a shirt or a cardigan over a dress—you can easily take it off if you get too overheated. Additionally, layers allow you to mix and match pieces to create a variety of appearances with the same clothing.

NOT TO BE OVERLOOKED is the bag. A purse that is both roomy enough to hold all of your necessities and fashionable enough to go with your ensemble is what you need. A stylish backpack or an organized tote can be useful and stylish at the same time. Additionally, keep in mind that a bag should complement your entire ensemble because it is more than just a place to hold your belongings.

THE KEY TO STRIKING a balance between appearance and functionality is to make wise decisions. One does not have to be given up for the other. It's about figuring out what suits your body, your

STYLING SUCCESS : HOW TO BUILD A WARDROBE THAT REFLECTS YOUR AMBITIONS

workspace, and you. And never forget that wearing power clothing is about feeling confident and prepared to take on the world, not about being uncomfortable.

THAT'S ALL THERE IS to it, ladies. Beyond simply looking good, power dressing is about making an impression, gaining respect, and positioning oneself for success. It's all about selecting items that bolster your confidence, exude authority, and are functional enough to get you through the day. When you dress with intention, you are wearing for the job you desire rather than just the one you now hold. So go ahead, own your style, and let your clothes do the talking. You're capable.

From Meetings to Mingling: Transitioning Your Look

How to kill the game without missing a beat, from dawn to dusk, in the boardroom or the bar. We've all been in the situation where you should be enjoying cocktails at a networking event one minute and managing business like a boss in a conference room the next. The challenge exists, but what is the answer? It all comes down to becoming an expert at the day-to-night transition. You must be prepared to completely change the look of your appearance, going from polished socialite to professional without breaking a sweat. Let's examine how to transform that power suit into an evening wardrobe stealer in a few simple steps.

Daily-to-Night Clothes Ideas

Versatility is essential when choosing your outfit for a day where you'll be hopping from meeting to socializing. Something that says, "I'm here to celebrate it at 7 PM and I'm here to close the deal" at 10 AM is what you need.

Foremost things foremost, choose a sophisticated and timeless basic ensemble. Consider a classy jumpsuit, a pair of pants with a blouse that fits well, or a basic sheath dress. These are pieces that can easily be dressed up for a night out, yet they are still sufficiently professional to command respect in the workplace. The way you stack and accessorize these items is what creates the magic.

STYLING SUCCESS : HOW TO BUILD A WARDROBE THAT REFLECTS YOUR AMBITIONS

THE TRUTH IS, THE LESS clothes you have to change, the better. After hours, the last thing you want to do is carry around a complete new wardrobe only to change up your appearance. Rather, concentrate on components that can be altered with minimal adjustments. For example, a sheath dress can be dressed up or down with a simple shoe and jacket change and a bold lip color. The fitted pants you've been wearing all day? You're set to make an impression if you wear them with a striking necklace and a great pair of heels.

For adaptability, neutral colors like gray, black, and navy are your greatest friends. They serve as a blank canvas on which you can add accessories and striking embellishments to create an evening masterpiece. However, don't feel that you have to stick to the neutrals; if a striking color or pattern appeals to you, go for it. Just make sure it doesn't feel very office-like and can easily transition into the evening.

Incorporating accessories for versatility

Your secret weapon for transitioning your look from business to social events is an accessory. Without having to fully redecorate your closet, the appropriate accessories can drastically alter the feel of your ensemble and give it a brand-new feel.

For the evening, change up your look from your daytime faves of low heels or flats to a statement pair of heels or ankle boots. The additional height immediately adds a touch of glitz and self-assurance. And don't be afraid to take risks when it comes to your shoe selection. Whether it's a striking texture, a splash of color, or a hint of glitter, your shoes have the power to elevate any ensemble.

JEWELRY IS THE NEXT topic. Here's where you can let your personality shine through and have a great time. You could wear a delicate necklace or simple studs during the day. However, replace those with a bright necklace, a big bracelet, or statement earrings when it's time to socialize. Contrast is crucial in this situation; if your ensemble is sleek and basic, your accessories should be the main attraction. If you've been acting cautiously all day, it's time to step it up or shut up.

Not to be overlooked is the influence of a well-chosen purse. You might fit all of your necessities in a stylish backpack or an organized bag that you wear during the day. However, for the evening, go for something cuter and more fashionable. A clutch, a chic crossbody bag, or even a bag with metallic accents will work well. Only the necessities to keep you feeling and looking amazing should fit in your evening bag.

BUT WHAT IS THE IDEAL piece of clothing to wear from day to night? The jacket must be that. A workplace setting is ideal for a blazer or structured jacket since it exudes professionalism, refinement, and a sense of business. However, that same blazer might be the final detail that really makes your evening look stunning when the clock strikes six o'clock. Alternatively, you might exchange that blazer for a shawl, a statement coat, or even a leather jacket if you want to change things up. The appropriate outer layer may totally change the look of your ensemble by bringing in edge, elegance, or any other desired mood.

Getting Ready for Unexpected Occurrences with Style

You're familiar with these situations: the unexpected client meeting that develops into an evening out; the last-minute dinner invitation; the spontaneous happy hour. You have to be prepared for everything, sis, which means carrying along a few necessities to make sure you're always set to go from day to night, no matter what.

Always carry an extra pair of shoes. By afternoon, those pumps you were so certain about this morning could become painful. Just in case, keep a change of stylish yet comfy flats or sandals in your car or purse. When anything unforeseen occurs, they'll rescue your feet and keep you looking fashionable.

STYLING SUCCESS : HOW TO BUILD A WARDROBE THAT REFLECTS YOUR AMBITIONS

Makeup comes next. Applying a quick touch-up before leaving for work can have a significant impact. To freshen up your look, carry a compact makeup bag containing the necessities: mascara, powder, lipstick, and possibly some eyeliner. A dramatic lip may instantly transform your appearance from day to night, and a fast dusting of powder can keep you appearing put together.

And sis, never undervalue the impact of a tiny perfume spritz. Before you leave, grab a travel-sized bottle of your favorite fragrance to give yourself a little pick-me-up. A well-chosen scent has the power to uplift your spirits and make an impact.

NOT TO BE OVERLOOKED is hair. Think about putting your hair down for the evening if it has been up all day. A fast hairdo change can completely change the way you look. Try using a handheld curling iron to give a little wave or curl to your normally straight hair. Alternatively, if your hair has been down, put it up into a chic bun or ponytail. The secret is to make just enough of a change to your appearance to feel like you've changed.

Lastly, always have a standout piece ready. This could be a striking pair of earrings, a statement necklace, or a vibrant scarf. Something that declares, "I'm ready for the night," something you can throw on at the last minute. When you need to make a quick transition, having that go-to piece might be life-saving. It's the simple things that matter the most.

And there you have it. It need not be difficult to go from meetings to socializing. Whatever your day—or night—throws at you, you can effortlessly and fashionably transform your look with the correct tactics. Recall that it all comes down to adaptability, astute accessorizing, and being ready for anything. Your wardrobe should be as adaptable as you are, enabling you to change directions and tackle any task head-on. So go ahead and master the shift from day to night. You can succeed at this!

All this, is a beautiful walk to the pages of Princella's style and power, you too can!

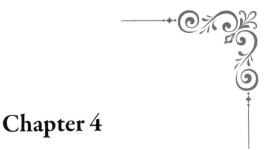

Chapter 4

Elevating Your Wardrobe with Accessories

The Role of Accessories in Personal Style

If there's one thing I know for sure about Princella, girl, it's that the little details make all the difference in an ensemble. They may quickly transform your appearance from plain to amazing by adding that extra flair, personality, or something special that makes you stand out from the crowd. Consider accessories as the flavoring in your outfit—the appropriate quantity can turn an outfit from boring to amazing. And believe me, nobody likes to present a boring appearance. Let's explore how accessories might help you express your true self and dress more stylishly.

Suggested Accessory Selections to Complement Your Outfit

The key to selecting accessories is understanding what suits you best. You cannot simply put on anything and hope it works. No, sis. You have to use it deliberately. Similar to the ideal spice on your favorite dish, the proper accessory can make your entire ensemble look put together. It all comes down to harmony, balance, and a hint of audacity.

How does it feel? Which style—bold and daring, relaxed and easygoing, or classic chic—are you going for? Accessory items ought to correspond with that vibe. Maybe you choose a bold necklace that catches the light as you walk to go with your chic black dress. Alternatively, if you're going casual with jeans and a tee, stacked necklaces or a stylish belt might offer the perfect amount of intrigue. The secret is to let your accessories enhance rather than overshadow your ensemble.

Color is something you now need to think about. If you're wearing mostly neutral hues, accessories are a terrific way to inject some color into your ensemble. But take caution not to go overboard. It's important not to appear overly forced. A striking scarf, a bold red lip, or a striking pair of earrings can be all it takes to elevate your ensemble. But keep in mind that less is more, sis. Allow one or two pieces to stand out if they resonate with you.

ADDITIONALLY, KEEP proportion in mind. To maintain balance when wearing an item with a lot of volume, such as a flowy dress or a thick sweater, opt for more delicate accessories. Conversely, if your outfit is sleek and fitting, you may afford to accessorise more extravagantly. Consider wearing a massive necklace, a statement cuff, or enormous hoops. It all comes down to experimenting with contrast and making sure your accessories complete your style rather than drawing attention away from it.

Above all, pick compositions that speak to you. Your accessories ought to be a representation of your distinct style and an extension of who you are. Don't be averse to showcasing your assertive and self-assured persona through your accessories. It's okay if you like a more relaxed, minimalist look; just make sure your accessories have a big impression without being overt. The most crucial factor is that you should feel confident in your clothing. Since you appear good while you're feeling nice. And that's the ultimate aim, my friend.

Conversation Pieces vs. Daily Needs

Now that we've established the distinction between statement pieces and everyday basics, let's get started. Both have a place in your closet, but you need to know when to go all out and when to play it safe.

Your wardrobe's show-stoppers are statement pieces. They are striking, audacious, and attention-grabbing. Imagine them as a band's

STYLING SUCCESS : HOW TO BUILD A WARDROBE THAT REFLECTS YOUR AMBITIONS

lead singer, commanding attention by taking center stage. Statement pieces are all about creating an impression, whether it's with a large set of chandelier earrings, a patterned scarf that makes a statement, or a massive necklace that demands attention.

THE PROBLEM IS THAT you can't wear a statement garment every single day. You could, of course, but it's not always feasible. The greatest times to wear statement pieces are when you want to stand out, leave a lasting impression, or simply feel like a total badass. They're your go-to tactic when you want to draw attention or when you need a little extra confidence boost.

However, daily necessities are the mainstay of your accessory collection. These are the things that you can wear with almost anything and that give your outfit the final touch without having to think twice. Consider a timeless watch, a delicate gold necklace, or your most beloved pair of hoops earrings. They're easy to wear, multipurpose, and always in style.

THE MAIN GOALS OF DAILY necessities are convenience and usefulness. They are the finishing touches to your outfit that never draw attention to themselves. Similar to a band's bassist, they are dependable, solid, and vital, yet they aren't always the center of attention. These items are essential to have in your wardrobe since they serve as the cornerstone of your accessory collection. When you need to seem put together but are in a hurry to get out the door, these are the first things you grab.

DON'T BE MISLED, THOUGH; just because something is referred to as vital doesn't imply it has to be dull. Your regular items can still provide you with enjoyment. Consider using tiny details, intriguing textures, or a hint of glitter. Finding the ideal mix between style and simplicity is key to wearing them every day without growing tired of them.

So what should you learn from this? Your accessory collection should include both striking pieces and everyday necessities. Your wow factor pieces are the ones you pull out when you want to create a big impression. Your dependable, constant companions that keep you looking put together and stylish no matter what are your everyday basics. The secret to upping your accessory game and guaranteeing that your appearance is always on point is knowing which to wear when.

The Art of Accessorizing: Minimalism vs. Maximalism

These are the two sides of the same coin, the yin and yang of the fashion industry. And, sis, it's critical to be aware of your stance on accessories since they reveal a lot about your sense of fashion and character.

The main tenets of minimalism are elegance, restraint, and simplicity. It is intended for the girl who like simple, elegant, and subtle design. As a minimalist, you most likely think that less is more. You don't like garish or ostentatious clothing. Rather, you want a few tasteful pieces that enhance your ensemble without drawing attention to themselves. Consider a basic leather belt, a tiny pair of stud earrings, or a gold bangle. These are the accessories that elevate a look without drawing attention to themselves.

Since the key to minimalism is knowing when to quit, it is an artistic endeavor. It all comes down to letting your inherent beauty and sense of style come through and selecting quality over quantity. When you want your ensemble to speak for itself without needing too much extra flare, the minimalist approach is ideal. It's elegant and effortless. Contrary to popular belief, minimalism does not equate to boredom. It just indicates that you've decided to let your accessories be subtle rather than overt.

Conversely, there is maximalism. And ladies, maximalism is a full-on roar if minimalism is a whisper. Maximalism is for the daring, the adventurous, the risk-takers in fashion who think that more really is more. It's all about layering, combining different textures, and making a bold statement. If you're a maximalist, you don't mind accessorizing excessively. How about wearing statement bags, stacked rings, layered necklaces, and huge earrings all together in one look? Sure, please!

Though it's a distinct form of art, maximalism is also an art form. It all comes down to styling a style that exudes vitality, charisma, and life. It's intended for the girl who wants to be seen, make a statement, and demonstrate to the world that she is a plaything. The trick with maximalism, though, is that balance is key. Despite adding a ton of accessories, you still need to take care that it doesn't become a heated mess. Between being assertive in a stylish way and being overly dramatic is a thin line. Thus, if you want to go maximalist, make sure your lunacy has a purpose.

You don't have to choose between minimalism and maximalism, which is fantastic. Depending on your disposition, the situation, or the attire, you can change it up. There are days when you want to go all out and make a statement, and days when you want to keep things simple and stylish. The secret is to be confident in your decisions and to know when and how to use each strategy.

Which one then are you? Are you a maximalist, a minimalist, or in the middle? Accessorizing is great since it allows you to express your individuality, style, and mood. You should always feel like the best version of yourself when wearing your accessories, whether you're stacking rings like there's no tomorrow or keeping it simple with just one piece. So go forth, lady, and accessorize your outfit with pieces that truly resonate with you. Because, in the end, how you wear something matters just as much as what you wear.

That's the tea, on how accessories can improve your wardrobe and help you achieve a more fashionable look like Princella. Whether you want to make a statement with standout items or keep things simple with everyday staples, it all comes down to recognizing what works for you. And never forget that feeling comfortable about what you're wearing matters more than being a maximalist, minimalist, or somewhere in between.

Chapter 5

Effective Buying Techniques

Shop Wisely: Prioritize Quality Above Quantity

LET'S FACE IT, DEPENDING on your approach, shopping may be a whole experience or a complete nightmare. Everything in the store seems to be begging for your attention as you walk in, but wait—are you really going to spend your money on everything? No. We're not that kind of people. We're talking about making wise wardrobe additions, prioritizing quality over quantity, and savvy buying. Let's examine how to identify high-quality textiles, why classic items are in style, and how to prevent impulsive purchases that will only make you regret your decision.

IDENTIFYING SUPERIOR Textiles and Structure

First things first: clothing ought to be well-made if you're going to spend your hard-earned money on it. I am referring to materials that do not pill after a single washing and edges that will not come apart by the end of the day. Creating a wardrobe that will last a lifetime requires understanding what constitutes high-quality apparel.

STYLING SUCCESS : HOW TO BUILD A WARDROBE THAT REFLECTS YOUR AMBITIONS

LET'S START WITH THE fabric. Get your hands dirty in the store instead than just reading the tag. Girl, feel the fabric! Does it have a pleasant weight and is it soft? Generally, you're better off sticking with natural fabrics like linen, cotton, wool, and silk. They feel opulent against your skin and are strong and breathable. Although synthetic materials like nylon and polyester have their uses, they don't always keep up as well—especially if you're seeking for a long-lasting item.

IT'S THE LITTLE THINGS that make a piece of high quality, therefore don't be scared to look closely at the seams. Do they have no loose threads and are they straight and tight? If necessary, turn the clothing inside out. There's no shame in ensuring sure the purchase is worthwhile. Additionally, inspect the hems. A garment that has been correctly hemmed will not have any exposed raw edges and will have a smooth finish that shows how much care was taken in its creation.

Despite their seeming tiny size, buttons and zippers are important markers of quality. Fake zippers can break or become stuck, and cheap buttons can come off after a few wears. Look for smooth-gliding zippers and robust, securely fastened buttons. Additionally, avoid sleeping on the lining; if something is lined, it was likely manufactured with care. Not only will a completely lined item appear better, but it will also be more comfortable and durable.

FINALLY, OBSERVE THE way a piece moves. Does it drape well or does it cling to everything in the wrong places when you try it on? A well-made garment should have some give to it so that it hangs nicely and accentuates your body. Place an item back on the rack if it seems fragile or like it will lose its shape after a few wears. You are worthy of better.

Purchasing Timeless Items vs. Purchases Driven by Trends

Let's talk about what to buy with your money now that you know how to recognize quality. It's simple to follow the newest fashions; while those neon bike shorts may be calling your name right now, will you still be in love with them in a year? Most likely not. It's crucial to invest in classic pieces that you can wear year-round and season after season for this reason.

Consider the essentials: a well-fitting jacket, a clean white shirt, a little black dress, and trousers. These are the items that your wardrobe is built around. Though they may not be the most ostentatious pieces, you will find yourself reaching for them repeatedly due to their adaptability, timeless appeal, and timeless quality. Purchasing these classic pieces means that you're creating a wardrobe that will work for you for many years to come, not just buying clothes.

LET'S FACE IT, THOUGH: trends may be entertaining. As long as you exercise caution while purchasing trendy items, there's nothing wrong with treating yourself occasionally. Balance is crucial. Spend no more than a portion of your money on fast fashion that will go out of style in a few months. Alternatively, add a few fashionable pieces to keep your wardrobe up to date and stylish. Make sure the item is something you truly adore and can see yourself wearing more than once, whether it's a unique print or a standout accessory.

Consider the cost per wear when looking for classic pieces. Although that $200 blazer can appear pricey at first, it will end up being a great deal if you wear it once a week for the next five years. However, what about that $20 shirt that ruins after just one wash? Not in that way. Buying items that will provide you with the best value over time is the main focus.

How an item fits into your current wardrobe is something else to take into account. Consider how you would wear it with your current wardrobe while you are shopping. It's probably an excellent buy if it complements at least three or four other pieces in your closet. But before you hand over your card, give it some thought if it's a one-hit wonder that will require you to purchase a complete new wardrobe.

Going Shopping with a Goal: How to Steer Clear of Impulse Buys

We've all been there: you're browsing your favorite online store or meandering through the mall then all of a sudden, there it is. That item that, until that very moment, you had no idea you needed. Let's speak about how to avoid making impulsive purchases that leave you broke and with a closet full of clothing you never wear, but hold on before you click "Add to Cart."

Initially, make a plan. Examine your clothing thoroughly before heading out to purchase. What is it that you really need? Do you need a decent pair of black pants for work? Do you require a new coat for winter? Create a list of the things you want to be sure to look for and follow it. This will assist you in maintaining concentration and preventing distraction from the bright new objects that constantly appear.

BUDGETING IS ANOTHER piece of advice. When shopping, especially when everything is on sale and you're in the mood for it, it's easy to get carried away. You don't have to buy something simply because it's on sale, though. Before you go shopping, make a budget for yourself to help you remain on target and avoid going overboard.

Consider this when you see something you like: Do I really need this? Will I wear it again in the future? Does it go with everything else in my closet? It is probably preferable to move on if any of these questions have a negative response. Give yourself some time to consider it if you're still not convinced. When making an internet purchase, wait a day or two before deciding what to buy. If you're in a store, leave and check if an hour later you're still thinking about it. When you're ready to buy, it will still be there if it's meant to be.

Prioritizing quality above quantity is another tactic. Although it can be alluring to stock up on cheap goods just because they're on sale, keep in mind that you're creating a wardrobe, not just accumulating stuff for your closet. In the long term, a few well-made, multipurpose pieces will be far more useful to you than a large number of flimsy, trendy pieces.

Finally, consider your own particular style. Something may not be appropriate for you just because it looks good on a mannequin or your favorite influencer. Remain loyal to items that give you a sense of comfort and confidence, and don't be hesitant to reject trends that don't fit your personal aesthetic.

STYLING SUCCESS : HOW TO BUILD A WARDROBE THAT REFLECTS YOUR AMBITIONS

Creating a wardrobe that represents who you are and makes you feel beautiful every time you get dressed is the goal of shopping, which is more than simply a way to kill time. You can create a wardrobe that not only looks nice but also lasts a lifetime by prioritizing quality over quantity, making timeless purchases, and going shopping with a purpose. Thus, keep these suggestions in mind the next time you go shopping and behave like the royalty that you are.

Setting a Budget for Your Clothes

Okay, sis. Let's speak about budgeting, which is a topic we don't often enjoy talking about but absolutely must. I realize that the term "budget" may make you shudder, but trust me when I say that it's essential to maintaining an impeccable wardrobe without going over budget. All of us want to look well, but we also have aspirations and money to pay. How therefore do we strike a balance? Let's explore how to make a budget for clothing that suits you, where to save, where to splurge, and how to find those deals without sacrificing quality.

Building a Budget for Fashion That Matches Your Financial Objectives

You must first and foremost be aware of your financial circumstances. Those expenses will come due, and you don't want to be caught off guard, so you can't just swipe your card and hope for the best. Now, let's talk honestly about your money. Examine your income, expenses, and savings objectives thoroughly first. How much can you actually budget each month for your wardrobe without jeopardizing your other financial objectives?

Having a clear image is the first step in creating a budget. But before you decide on a figure, consider how much you truly need and want to spend on clothing. Perhaps you enjoy shopping according to the seasons and change your clothes a few times a year. Or perhaps monthly hauls are all that matter to you. Make sure your budget matches your style, whatever it may be.

STYLING SUCCESS : HOW TO BUILD A WARDROBE THAT REFLECTS YOUR AMBITIONS

Generally speaking, you should budget between 5 and 10% of your monthly salary for your wardrobe. However, this isn't fixed, so feel free to increase that amount if you're a style icon who enjoys treating yourself to a bit extra spending. Just watch out that it doesn't interfere with your other budgetary priorities. Your goal is not to go broke, but to appear good.

THIS IS WHERE IT REALLY gets serious: follow your spending plan. When shopping, it's easy to get carried away, especially if you see something that you simply *have* to have. But keep in mind that adhering to your spending plan demonstrates your respect for your financial objectives and positions you for long-term success. And that is far more fulfilling than making any impulsive purchase, my friend.

Consider tracking your spending with a basic spreadsheet or a budgeting software to help you stay on target. Keep a log of all the purchases you make. In this manner, you'll always be aware of your situation and able to modify your spending as necessary. I promise you that controlling your expenditures gives you more power than allowing them rule you.

Spending Points and Savings Areas

Now that your budget is set up, let's consider strategy. Not every item in a closet is made equal when it comes to construction. While you can certainly save money on some products, there are some that are truly worth spending a lot of money on. The secret is to know when to save and when to splurge.

The indulgences. These are the staple pieces that will make up your entire wardrobe—items you'll wear year after year. I'm referring to a timeless trench coat, a well fitted jacket that fits like a dream, or a timeless pair of black shoes that go with everything. Since you want them to last, these are the parts that should be of the highest caliber.

When you indulge, choose classic and adaptable styles. Opt for muted hues that work well with everything in your wardrobe. Furthermore, don't be scared to spend money on high-quality fabrics like leather, silk, or wool. In the long run, they will seem more opulent and stand up better, even though they may initially cost more. Plus, there's something that gives you the confidence to take on the world when you slide into a well-made piece.

There's no need to spend a fortune on items that might go out of style the following year because trends come and go. It's all about having fun with trendy stuff without going over budget. Check fast-fashion stores or even thrift stores for reasonably priced replicas of the newest trends. In this manner, you can test a trend without having to make a large financial commitment.

Another place where you can cut costs is on accessories. While a luxury handbag is undoubtedly an investment worth making, you may find more affordable alternatives for everyday accessories like belts, scarves, and costume jewelry. These inexpensive accessories can give your ensemble a little personality boost.

NOT TO MENTION ESSENTIALS like tank tops, t-shirts, and casual attire. These are products that are typically less expensive without significantly compromising on quality. Try to find discounts at mid-range stores, or even think about purchasing in bulk during sales. Not everything that is fundamental has to be uninteresting or unattractive. If you style it correctly, a well-fitting, inexpensive t-shirt can look just as nice as a fancy one.

A Guide to Deal-Seeking Without Compromising Quality

Okay, so you know when to save and when to indulge, but how do you go about getting those deals? Considering that, who doesn't enjoy finding a deal? Finding discounts without compromising quality is crucial. Here's how to go about doing that.

STYLING SUCCESS : HOW TO BUILD A WARDROBE THAT REFLECTS YOUR AMBITIONS

Time is crucial. Although there are always sales at retailers, the amount you save can vary significantly depending on when you purchase. End-of-season bargains are a treasure trove for finding premium goods for a much lower cost. You may be purchasing a winter coat in March, but you will be happy that you did when December rolls around. The same is true for summer outfits in September; when the warm weather returns, you'll have a brand-new wardrobe.

Getting newsletters and following your preferred brands on social media are two other pieces of advice. As a subscriber or follower, you'll receive unique discounts from brands and be the first to know about their future sales. Just be cautious not to let the sale lure you in; after all, a discount is only worthwhile if you truly need the item.

Additionally, don't discount sample deals and outlet stores. These are excellent locations to purchase designer goods at a significant savings. It's possible that some research will be necessary, but the results may be worthwhile. Just be cautious to continue inspecting for quality; certain outlet items may be lower-quality copies created especially for the outlet. Be sure to thoroughly examine them before making a purchase.

Another excellent technique to locate discounts is through online buying, particularly if you're prepared to perform some price comparison. Coupons can be found on websites like RetailMeNot or Honey, and price comparison tools like Google Shopping allow you to see what other stores are charging. Additionally, keep in mind used websites like The RealReal, Depop, and Poshmark. Gently worn designer items can be found for a small portion of their original cost, and since they are used, you are also helping the environment.

SPEAKING OF USED, THRIFT and consignment stores may be veritable gold mines for fashionistas on a tight budget. You may have to sift through a number of subpar products, but if you're patient, you can uncover some genuine jewels. What's the best thing, then? The excitement of the quest is what makes thrift shopping so enjoyable, so when you do locate the ideal item, you'll feel even more accomplished.

FINALLY, NEVER UNDERVALUE the ability to negotiate. Never be afraid to negotiate a little while you're shopping at a flea market,

STYLING SUCCESS : HOW TO BUILD A WARDROBE THAT REFLECTS YOUR AMBITIONS

thrift store, or even some boutique stores. Asking for a discount could be enough, particularly if you're purchasing numerous things or find a small defect in the item. Asking is always beneficial, and the worst thing they can answer is no.

Here you have it: a how-to tutorial on clothing budgeting like an expert. You may assemble a fashionable yet frugal wardrobe by setting up a fashion budget that fits your spending limits, learning when to save and when to splurge, and becoming an expert deal-hunter. Recall that being fashionable includes feeling good about yourself and your financial objectives in addition to looking nice. So go ahead, decide on a spending limit, and start dressing like the chic, well-mannered queen you are.

Chapter 6

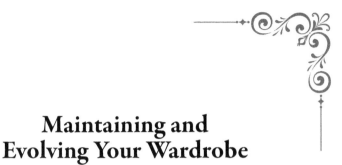

Maintaining and Evolving Your Wardrobe

Building a fantastic wardrobe is one thing, but maintaining it to keep it looking as wonderful as the day you acquired it is quite another. Since clothes are not inexpensive nor disposable, we must take care of them if we want them to continue serving us.

First, you should consider your clothing an investment. Since they are! That tiny black gown that gives you a royal feeling? Yes, you need to take care of it if you want that to endure. Now, I realize it's simple to throw everything in the washing on high heat and call it a day, but darling, it will quickly result in sweaters shrinking, colors fading, and textiles being damaged. What's the key to keeping your clothes looking new? It all comes down to care.

Don't just tear off and discard those care labels; instead, start by reading them! They teach you just how to handle each item, which is why they are there. Certain textiles require a delicate touch, which can be achieved by hand washing, utilizing a delicate cycle, or even washing them in cold water. Yes, it may take a bit longer, but when your garments retain their feel, color, and form, it will be well worth the effort. Not to be overlooked is drying. Your greatest ally is air drying. Dryers may be harsh on clothing, weakening fabrics, fading colors, and causing shrinkage. Thus, put up those fragile items and give them some natural airflow.

IT'S TIME FOR YOU TO organize your wardrobe, girl, if it's disorganized. In addition to being stressful, having a packed closet increases the likelihood that you will forget what you own and wear the same five items repeatedly. Invest on some high-quality hangers; wooden ones are ideal as they are robust and won't cause your clothing to lose its shape like those thin wire ones can. Stack your most used items at eye level so you can reach them quickly, and arrange everything according to category, matching outfits and pants, for example. It's much simpler to get dressed in the morning when you can see everything you have.

LET US NOT OVERLOOK the seasonal elements at this point. In the middle of July, who is wearing bulky wool sweaters? It is therefore time to rotate when the seasons change. Store your off-season clothing in breathable storage boxes to prevent musty smells, and make room for the outfits you will actually wear. However, make sure they are clean before putting them away! Over time, filth and stains on clothing can accumulate and become difficult to remove. Furthermore, pests like moths are less likely to be drawn to clean clothing. In addition, add

STYLING SUCCESS : HOW TO BUILD A WARDROBE THAT REFLECTS YOUR AMBITIONS

some cedar balls or lavender sachets to deter pests without giving off an offensive chemical odor.

You're doing them dirty if you're just brushing them off at the door and allowing them to pile up. Shoes also require maintenance! Make sure you rotate them frequently to avoid wearing the same pair every day, which might accelerate their wear and tear. To help them keep their shape, stuff them with shoe trees and occasionally give them a thorough cleaning and shine. Get a suede brush and apply a water and stain repellant to those kicks because suede requires specific care.

However, wardrobe care involves more than just keeping things tidy and orderly; it also involves understanding when to part with items. Everybody has certain items that they hoard in the hopes of wearing them again at some point. But girl, it's time to part ways if it's been in your closet for a year and you haven't worn it. Give it away, sell it, recycle it, but don't allow it occupy space that could be occupied by an item you truly adore and wear.

You may still occasionally change things up even when you have a strong base. Style should evolve with you, as fashion is all about expressing yourself. That doesn't mean you have to buy an entirely new wardrobe every season, but it does mean you should be willing to try new things, follow trends that interest you, and alter up your appearance when circumstances demand. Perhaps you've received a significant promotion and need to update your business attire. Alternatively, perhaps you're just noticing a change in yourself and you want your wardrobe to match. In any case, don't be scared to change.

BUT KEEP IN MIND THAT changing doesn't imply giving up on what makes sense for you. Store and construct upon those timeless things that you are certain you will return to time and time again. To keep your outfit fresh, add a few trendier pieces every season, but make sure they work well with what you currently own. Furthermore, don't hesitate to accessorize! An eye-catching jewelry, a striking bag, or a great pair of shoes may often completely transform an ensemble.

Don't underestimate the power of tailoring. Take it to a tailor and get it modified if something doesn't fit quite right instead of throwing it in the back of your wardrobe. The way an item fits and appears on you can be greatly altered with a small tweak here and there. Not only may suits benefit from tailoring, but dresses, skirts, slacks, and even jeans can also be made to fit a little better. Additionally, if anything you treasure is getting old and has to be fixed rather than being thrown away, do so. A skilled tailor has the ability to create magic, giving items you thought were finished new life.

Balance is key to updating and maintaining your outfit. It's about taking good care of your clothes to make them last and letting your style develop and change with you. It all comes down to recognizing what suits you and making sure that your wardrobe represents your current self rather than your past self from five years ago. Above all, wearing clothing that makes you feel good is crucial because confident people look good and project that feeling into everything they do.

Take good care of your clothes. If you give it the care it requires, it will continue to provide for you for many years to come. Recall that fashion is meant to be enjoyable. Instead of worrying about having the ideal closet, concentrate on creating one that makes you feel amazing every single day.

Maintaining Your Your Style

Now, let's talk about how to maintain a current appearance as the years pass. You know the story: life happens, and suddenly your wardrobe is everything you've ever wanted. Your closet full of clothes just doesn't seem to be hitting the same notes as it did to when your business takes off and your style starts to change. But, sis, don't worry. Regarding how to maintain that wardrobe changing with you, I've got you covered.

FIRST OF ALL, YOUR wardrobe should change along with your work. Business casual may be the norm when you first start out in an entry-level role, but suddenly, boom! As you advance in your career, you'll find yourself in rooms where the dress code is more "power player" than "office junior." This indicates that it's time to upgrade your wardrobe as well. You have to step it up and wear clothes that fit your current situation and future goals. You can't keep dressing in the same outfits you did when you first started.

WHAT MESSAGE DO YOU want your clothing to convey? is a question you must ask yourself. You should dress in a way that communicates your newfound leadership. Don't let the "I'm in charge" vibe be overshadowed by striking accessories, structured blazers, and tailored suits, though. If you've always been drawn to striking prints, don't let that enthusiasm die; instead, find ways to enrich the look. Perhaps it's a well-fitting dress with a striking design or a killer pair of heels that give your ensemble a splash of color. To change without losing the essence of what makes your style uniquely you is the aim.

TRENDS. EVEN THOUGH they come and go more quickly than the newest TikTok challenge, you shouldn't completely disregard them. Keeping your look modern and fresh may be achieved by incorporating trends into your wardrobe, but the key is to do so without sacrificing your sense of style. Choose a few items that speak to you and work them into your current wardrobe instead of going all out and purchasing every trendy thing you see on Instagram.

Go for it, for instance, if you think that wearing an enormous blazer suits your style. However, rather of going all out trendy, you may go for a classic cut blazer that fits slightly too large. In this manner, you can follow the trend without deviating too much from who you are. If you've always loved animal print and it's hot right now, find a way to wear it subtly and stylishly, such with a snakeskin purse or a leopard print belt. Finding the right balance between following the latest trends and remaining authentic is crucial.

However, let's face it: occasionally, a wardrobe makeover isn't enough. Sometimes a thorough cleansing is necessary. Yes, I did say that. There comes a point at which you have to part with the components that aren't serving you anymore. Everybody has certain things in their closet that they are clinging to despite knowing they are well beyond their sell-by date. It's time to say goodbye to things, like that dress you wore to your cousin's wedding and haven't touched since, or that pair of trousers that fit great five years ago but not so much now.

STYLING SUCCESS : HOW TO BUILD A WARDROBE THAT REFLECTS YOUR AMBITIONS

IT'S CRUCIAL TO KNOW when to let go. It's probably time to part with it if you're not wearing it and it doesn't make you happy (yeah, I'm getting all Marie Kondo on you). Furthermore, it's about creating room in your life for new items that represent who you are today, not just organizing your closet. Consider it a sort of closet purge where you get rid of items to create place for new ones.

Hey, I understand; it's not easy to let go. Perhaps that item holds sentimental significance for you, or you're positive you'll wear it again sometime. The truth is, you need to face the music if you haven't worn it in more than a year. If it's a fine piece, think about selling it or giving it to a worthy recipient. Should it have seen better days, it might be time to recycle it. Don't just let it take up space, whatever you do. We want to convey the fresh enthusiasm that comes with a new clothing.

NOW, REMEMBER TO MAINTAIN your wardrobe's functionality as you update it over time. Your needs also change as your life does. You may require more adaptable clothing that can be worn in many conditions or that can go from day to night if you travel frequently for work. You may discover that you require more comfortable yet fashionable clothing and fewer formal things if you work from home. It all comes down to adjusting to your current situation and making sure that your clothes work for you rather than against you.

NOT TO BE OVERLOOKED is the ability of accessories to update your appearance. Occasionally, a stylish handbag, a striking necklace, or a fresh pair of earrings are all that are needed to revitalize an ensemble. The simplest method to alter your appearance without having to completely redecorate your closet is using accessories. They're also a fantastic way to try out trends without committing too much.

Are you unsure if the trend of neon colors is for you? Before committing fully, try it out with a belt or a pair of shoes.

THE TRUTH IS, THOUGH, that updating your clothing over time involves more than just what you have in your closet. What matters is how you feel about your wardrobe. Your clothing should change to reflect whatever changes you're making in your life and profession. It ought to give you a sense of empowerment, confidence, and the ability to be the best version of yourself. Aligning your external appearance with your inner self and future goals is the essence of updating your look.

So, don't be scared to change things around as you go through different stages of life. Accept change, try out different looks, and above all, be loyal to who you are. Since fashion is all about expressing oneself, your wardrobe ought to represent you at every turn in life. Maintain it unique, enjoyable, and you. And never forget—you can do this!

Building Confidence Through Your Wardrobe

There's more to your wardrobe than just the clothes you keep in your closet, sis. The items that enable you to walk into the world and declare, "I'm here, and I'm about to own this day," are your armor, your combat gear. But how do you develop that self-assurance through your clothing choices? That is an art form, and it has the power to uplift you beyond anything else.

LET'S BE HONEST ABOUT what you're working with first things first. It's that simple: when you look nice, you feel wonderful. It's not just about looking good, though; it's also about clothing in a way that makes you move with purpose, stand taller, and draw attention to yourself without having to say anything. Something wonderful happens when you put on an outfit that fits well and enhances your body type, skin tone, and overall attitude. We're focusing on the energy that makes you feel like you can take on the world.

Knowing what makes you feel powerful is just as important to dressing to improve your self-esteem as knowing what to wear. Perhaps the extra lift comes from a fantastic pair of heels that uplifts your mood as much as your body. Perhaps it's that blazer that makes you feel like the boss you are—it fits your shoulders like it was built just for you.

Whatever it is, you should identify the items in your wardrobe that give you that unstoppable feeling and then embrace them.

But wait—how you wear your clothes matters just as much as the items themselves when it comes to confidence. Owning your appearance is crucial. You have to put on whatever you're wearing and walk out looking like the coolest person on the neighborhood. Because, let's face it, confidence originates from inside, and everything you wear is merely a mirror of that strength. Everyone will think you look nice if you think so yourself. Rock that ensemble as like it were meant for you, because it sort of was.

Have you ever noticed how some clothes give you the confidence to tackle any task? This is due to the fact that clothing can alter your perspective. You're putting yourself in a successful position when you choose clothing that makes you feel powerful, attractive, and capable. When you put on that ideal clothing, it's like a mental switch flipping—you stop doubting yourself and start believing you can face any challenge that comes your way.

So tell me, how do you empower yourself with your wardrobe? Sort through your closet and choose clothes that best represent who you are. Finding what makes you feel like the queen that you are is more important than following trends or dressing like everyone else. Maybe it's the fitted, sleek items that give you that additional edge, or maybe it's the vibrant hues that make you feel alive. Organize your clothing based on that item.

STYLING SUCCESS : HOW TO BUILD A WARDROBE THAT REFLECTS YOUR AMBITIONS

Also, don't be scared to try new things. Pushing your limits, taking risks, and venturing outside of your comfort zone are all ways to become more empowered. Therefore, if your style has always been safe, it might be time to take a chance. Try those quirky patterned jeans you weren't sure you could pull off or that bright red dress you've been eyeing. The truth is that when you challenge yourself to try different looks, you're also challenging yourself to develop, and that's where real empowerment originates.

HOWEVER, WE MUST NOT overlook the significance of consistently honing your style as an indicator of your own development. As you change, so should your style. It's acceptable if the clothing that gave you confidence five years ago don't have the same impact on you now. Your wardrobe should expand to fit your growing body. It entails periodically assessing the items in your wardrobe and asking yourself, "Does this still represent who I am?"

Being sincere with yourself about your current situation and future goals will help you refine your style. Your outfit should be a reflection of your professional advancement. Your clothing should convey that you are starting a new chapter in your life. It's okay to part with items that no longer serve you. Clothes that don't fit the person you're becoming should be thrown away, just as you wouldn't hang onto bad habits that don't support your goals.

And, never undervalue the influence accessories have on enhancing your wardrobe's ability to project confidence. The correct accessories can instantly transform an outfit from plain to amazing. Consider how a beautiful handbag can complete a look or how a bold necklace can add flair to a basic garment. Accessorizing can easily elevate your confidence without having to completely redecorate your clothing, since they serve as the final touches that complete your style.

The secret is to wear accessories for more reasons than merely being in style or being told they look good by others. Put them on because they lift your spirits. Select accessories that elevate your style and help you feel like the greatest version of yourself, whether it's a delicate bracelet that adds a touch of refinement to your ensemble or a pair of enormous hoops earrings that make you feel fierce.

WEARING SOMETHING THAT truly represents you on the outside is the epitome of empowerment. It all comes down to authenticity, staying loyal to who you are, and refusing to try to fit into the model of someone else. You truly start to shine when your wardrobe is a reflection of who you are.

So how can one develop that kind of self-assurance? Start by figuring out what makes you special and how to use your style to convey that. Perhaps you're all about bright colors and statement prints, or perhaps you like simpler, monochrome styles. Accept it for what it is. Never be scared to make an impression or to stand out. Wear your style with pride, as it is a reflection of who you are, what you've been through, and how you've traveled.

And never forget that confidence is something you develop over time rather than something you're born with. It works similarly to a muscle that gains strength with continued use. Thus, begin modestly—perhaps with a piece that's a touch outside your comfort zone—and progressively challenge yourself to attempt novel experiences. It will become simpler to create a wardrobe that expresses your confidence and empowerment the more you try new things and learn what those things are.

ULTIMATELY, HAVING confidence comes down to feeling good about yourself and letting your clothes reflect that. It's about being authentic and refusing to let other people tell you how to dress or look. So go forth, own your style and let your clothing to represent the strong, self-assured woman you are. You can do anything when you feel confident in your attire.

Style and Achievement

What comes to mind when you think of success? Is it the fancy car, the powerful position, or perhaps the large bank account? All of these can certainly play a role, but here's what I want you to know: success and style go hand in hand in unexpected ways. You see, the way you show yourself to the world has the power to make all the difference in the world—it can open doors, create chances, and establish the kind of success you're about to achieve.

NOT ONLY CAN STYLING make you look beautiful, but it may also make you feel good. When you believe you look the part, your perspective changes. People notice the confidence you emit, the higher you walk, and the clearer you speak. That is the power of style, and you may use it to motivate yourself to succeed.

THE SECRET TO SUCCESS is not just what you do, but also how you do it. And to be honest, your appearance has a role in that "how" as well. Before you even speak, the way you dress matters a lot, whether you're entering a boardroom, taking the stage, or even just turning up for an interview. It all comes down to establishing the correct mood, making the appropriate impression, and matching your appearance to your objectives.

Picture yourself giving a major presentation in a few days. Even though you're prepared and knowledgeable, there seems to be something lacking when you look in the mirror. Your style can help if you're lacking that spark or extra push that gives you confidence that you can succeed. The entire game can change with the appropriate attire. All of a sudden, you're not simply giving a presentation; you're in charge of the space. You are the owner of every word that leaves your mouth, not simply the speaker.

Furthermore, it goes beyond the significant occasions. You convey stories with your style every single day. The message is, "I'm here." I'm prepared. I'm serious about my success. Success requires consistency, which is about putting in a full effort each and every day. You must take yourself seriously if you want other people to do the same. It's about realizing that, in the eyes of the people who matter, the little things—like the way your shoes shine or the shape of your jacket—can sum up to enormous things.

TO BE CLEAR, THOUGH, successful styling does not entail dressing like everyone else. Since success is a personal matter, so should your style. It all comes down to figuring out what works for you and what inspires you to be your strongest self, then pursuing that path. Perhaps your strength comes from a striking outfit that makes you stand out in the best possible manner, or perhaps you're the type of person who feels unstoppable in a crisp suit. Accept it for what it is.

STYLING SUCCESS : HOW TO BUILD A WARDROBE THAT REFLECTS YOUR AMBITIONS

Being successful means standing out for all the right reasons, not just fitting in. It all comes down to standing out and making an impression that is deeper than meets the eye. Indeed, a significant factor in it is your style. People are drawn to genuineness that comes through when you are true to yourself and your own style.

HOWEVER, DRESSING WELL for success involves more than simply your wardrobe—it also involves your mindset. At the end of the day, style is more than just fabric and thread—it's about how those things make you feel. So, it's about putting on that dress and starting the day with the attitude, "I'm here to win." It's all about the motivation that comes from knowing you're prepared for anything comes your way and the confidence that comes from knowing you look the part.

Remember that success is about the journey as much as the destination. An element of the journey is your style, which changes as you go farther and higher. Your style develops with you, mirroring your personal development and the lessons you've learnt. It's a continuous, ever-changing process, much like success.

Thus, keep this in mind the next time you're considering your objectives, aspirations, and lofty dreams: your style is a tool, a weapon, and an essential component of the formula for success. It's something you have daily control over and can use to your advantage. There are no limits to what you can accomplish when you get it right and match your purpose and style.

ULTIMATELY, ALIGNMENT is the key to both success and style: ensuring that every aspect of your life is geared toward advancing your objectives. When your style and inner drive are in harmony, you become unstoppable. Your style is the external manifestation of your inner drive. At that point, success becomes something you embody, something you attract, and something you can proudly wear. It is no longer just something you chase.

So go ahead and dress to succeed. Because there's no reason you shouldn't enter that future looking like the boss you are, and you deserve to look as amazing as the future you're building.

A Note to the Contemporary Woman

It's time, ladies, to have a meaningful discussion about what it means to be a modern woman in the contemporary world. Today's world is one in which obstacles are being broken, ceilings are being broken, and the definition of success is being redefined. But let's face it, there are obstacles on this trip that must be overcome. You are expected to be aspirational, caring, robust, sensitive, fashionable, and not overly conceited all at once. It's a delicate balance, and occasionally it seems like everyone is observing you and hoping you'll make a mistake.

Let me tell you something, though: the modern woman strides instead of merely walking. She commands every square inch of the room that she takes up, and she does it with poise, assurance, and an unabashed sense of self. It's not about trying to fit into a stereotype that society has put forth for us. Here, you are going to break that mold and establish our own guidelines.

Your aspirations, dreams, and objectives surpass any boundaries that others may attempt to impose upon you. Having aspirations like those necessitates projecting an image of oneself that is strong, wise, and imaginative. Success is about more than just our accomplishments; it's about the way we conduct ourselves every day. It's about stepping out into the world with a purpose and a demeanor that exudes confidence in one's identity and direction.

Being a modern lady isn't always simple. You attempt to please everyone by balancing several responsibilities and being loyal to who you are. It's draining, and sometimes we just need a gentle reminder that it's acceptable to put our needs, wants, and objectives first.

I THUS GIVE YOU THIS advice, modern lady: don't be scared to shine. Never allow somebody to make you feel less than wonderful or that you're too much. You are perfect in your own skin. Your aspirations are genuine, your objectives are attainable, and your style—yes, your style—is a potent weapon that you can employ to confidently navigate this world.

DON'T DRESS LIKE THE boss you want to be; instead, dress like the boss you are. Allow your appearance to speak for you every day when you go out, even before you speak a word. Show the world that you are here to take action, change the world, and leave your mark.

AND NEVER FORGET THAT style is about expressing oneself, not about following trends or labels. Wearing what gives you a sense of strength, beauty, and unstoppability is key. Own it, whether it's a statement lip, a striking coat, or your go-to heels. Allow your sense of style to convey your fortitude, tenacity, and unwavering self-assurance.

STYLING SUCCESS : HOW TO BUILD A WARDROBE THAT REFLECTS YOUR AMBITIONS

You have the ability to write the story of your own lives as contemporary women. You are free to define success as you see it and to pursue it in the ways that best suit you. Therefore, never listen to someone who says you can't have it all. You'll be able to and will. But keep in mind that having it all does not entail going it alone. Rely on your community, your tribe, and your sisters. Remember that you are unstoppable when you band together, encourage one another, and recognize one other's accomplishments.

So, modern lady, get out there and kill it. Whether you're pursuing your goals, managing a boardroom, or raising a family, always remember to do it with style, enthusiasm, and, above all, love for yourself. Because your relationship with yourself is ultimately the most significant one you have. Take care of it, treasure it, and let it serve as the cornerstone around which your prosperity is constructed.

Being authentic is the most powerful thing you can do in a world where people are always attempting to tell you who you should be. This one's for you, modern lady: may you always radiate your truth, walk in your strength, and style your accomplishment with unabashed confidence. Take it; the world is yours.

Conclusion

OKAY, THIS STYLING success trip has taken us a long way, haven't it? We've covered a wide range of topics, including the influence of smart purchasing, tailoring, and accessorizing in addition to the power of a well-curated wardrobe. The truth is that style has everything to do with self-discovery as much as it does with fashion.

Your clothing collection? It's your narrative, your armor, and your expression. Every item you select and every look you put together represents who you are and where you want to go. Contrary to popular belief, style also involves feeling good as well as looking nice. It all comes down to that confident swagger you get when you know you've put something together that gives you the impression that you can take on the world.

STYLING SUCCESS : HOW TO BUILD A WARDROBE THAT REFLECTS YOUR AMBITIONS

I want you to take a moment to review what you've learned as we come to an end. Consider the changes in your thinking, the fresh viewpoints you've acquired, and the way you've begun to view fashion as a tool—a means for self-love, empowerment, and success—rather than merely a necessary.

Don't, however, stop reading these pages with this information. Use it. Enjoy it. Allow it to change not only your clothes but also the way you live. Let your look convey that you are a boss, whether you're cruising about the house, heading out to brunch with your pals, or entering a boardroom.

And keep in mind, sweetie, that possessing an enormous wardrobe is not the goal. It all comes down to having a closet full of items that exude confidence and declare to the world, "I know who I am, and I'm not afraid to show it." So go ahead and flaunt your self-assurance by dressing like a boss and wearing that exquisitely tailored jacket. Make a statement with your style even before you speak a word.

THE CONTEMPORARY WOMAN in this world creates trends rather than merely following them. She is unique; she doesn't just blend in. And you're going to do precisely that. You're going to leave here with a stronger sense of personal style, a better comprehension of what it means to dress for success, and—above all—unwavering self-assurance.

Thus, continue to shine, to kill, and to style your success like the queen that you are. You should walk down the globe as if you own it, because you really do, sis.

Cheers to you, your accomplishments, and a time when style signifies more than simply clothes—it's about confidence, strength, and purpose. Continue taking action, keep shattering stereotypes, and never lose sight of the fact that you are an unstoppable modern women—not just a lady.

keep feisty, keep fabulous, and most of all, be authentic. Your success story in style is just getting started. Go forth now and finish writing it in your own distinctive, fearless, and oh-so-stylish style.

Don't miss out!

Visit the website below and you can sign up to receive emails whenever Gordon Mills publishes a new book. There's no charge and no obligation.

https://books2read.com/r/B-A-CWUEC-TCDNE

BOOKS 2 READ

Connecting independent readers to independent writers.

Milton Keynes UK
Ingram Content Group UK Ltd.
UKHW022026230824
447344UK00012B/788